Praise for *Growth Hacker Marketing*

"Growth hackers are the new VPs of marketing, and this book tells you how to make the transformation."

—Andrew Chen, Silicon Valley
entrepreneur, essayist, and startup advisor

"This book is a wake-up call for every marketing exec in the business. And a tutorial for engineers, IT, founders, and designers. Read it."

—Porter Gale, former VP of Marketing
at Virgin America and author of
Your Network Is Your Net Worth

"Finally, a crystallization and explanation of growth hacking in easy-to-understand terms—and better, real strategies and tactics for application."

—Alex Korchinski, director of growth at Soma

"Holiday is part Machiavelli, part Ogilvy, and all results. . . . This whiz kid is the secret weapon you've never heard of."

—Timothy Ferriss, author of *The 4-Hour Workweek*

GROWTH HACKER MARKETING

Ryan Holiday is a media strategist and prominent writer on strategy and business. After dropping out of college at nineteen to apprentice under Robert Greene, author of *The 48 Laws of Power*, he went on to advise many bestselling authors and multiplatinum musicians. He served as director of marketing at American Apparel for many years, where his campaigns have been used as case studies by Twitter, YouTube, and Google and written about in *AdAge*, the *New York Times*, and *Fast Company*.

His first book, *Trust Me, I'm Lying: Confessions of a Media Manipulator*—which the *Financial Times* called "an astonishing, disturbing book"—was a debut bestseller and is now taught in colleges around the world. He is currently an editor at large for the *New York Observer* and contributes to *Thought Catalog* from his home in Austin, Texas.

Ryanholiday.net
@ryanholiday

GROWTH HACKER MARKETING

A Primer on the Future of PR,

Marketing, and Advertising

RYAN HOLIDAY

PROFILE BOOKS

First published in Great Britain in 2014 by
PROFILE BOOKS LTD
3A Exmouth House
Pine Street
London EC1R 0JH
www.profilebooks.com

First published in the United States of America in 2013 in digital format
in 2013 by Portfolio / Penguin, A Penguin Random House Company

This expanded edition published in 2014

10 9 8 7 6

Printed and bound in Great Britain by
CPI Group (UK) Ltd, Croydon, CR0 4YY

A CIP catalogue record for this book is available from the British Library.

ISBN 978 1 78125 436 3
eISBN 978 1 78283 019 1

The paper this book is printed on is certified by the © 1996 Forest Stewardship
Council A.C. (FSC). It is ancient-forest friendly. The printer holds FSC chain of
custody SGS-COC-2061

I prefer the discipline of knowledge to the anarchy of ignorance. We pursue knowledge the way a pig pursues truffles.

—DAVID OGILVY

CONTENTS

AN INTRODUCTION TO GROWTH HACKING *xiii*

STEP 1

IT BEGINS WITH PRODUCT MARKET FIT *1*

STEP 2

FINDING YOUR GROWTH HACK *15*

STEP 3

TURN 1 INTO 2 AND 2 INTO 4—GOING VIRAL *31*

STEP 4

CLOSE THE LOOP: RETENTION AND OPTIMIZATION *43*

CONTENTS

**MY CONVERSION: PUTTING THE
LESSONS INTO PRACTICE** *57*

SPECIAL BONUS *69*

AFTERWORD *71*

A GROWTH HACKING GLOSSARY *79*

FAQS *91*

**BECOMING A GROWTH HACKER:
THE NEXT STEPS** *101*

ACKNOWLEDGMENTS *107*

NOTES *109*

AN INTRODUCTION
TO GROWTH HACKING

Nearly two years ago now, on what seemed like a normal day, I got in my car to leave my house, assuming it would be no different from any other workday. I had read the morning news, dealt with a few important employee issues over the phone, and confirmed lunch and drinks meetings for later in the day. I headed to the athletic club—a swanky, century-old private gym favored by downtown executives—and swam and ran and then sat in the steam room to think.

As I entered the office around ten, I nodded to my assistant and sat down at a big desk and reviewed all the papers that required my signature. There were ad designs to approve, invoices to process, events to sponsor, proposals to review. A new product was launching, and I had a press release to write. A stack of magazines had arrived— I handed them to an employee to catalog and organize for the press library.

My job: director of marketing at American Apparel. I had a half dozen employees working under me in my office. Right across the hall from us, thousands of sewing machines were humming away, manned by the world's most efficient garment workers. A few doors down was a photo studio where the very ads I would be placing were made.

Excepting the help of a few pieces of technology, like my computer and smartphone, my day had begun and would proceed exactly as it had for every other marketing executive for the last seventy-five years. Buy advertisements, plan events, pitch reporters, design "creatives," approve promotions, and throw around terms like "brand," "CPM," "awareness," "earned media," "top of mind," "added value," and "share of voice." That was the job; that's always been the job.

I'm not saying I'm Don Draper or Edward Bernays or anything, but the three of us could probably have swapped offices and routines with only a few adjustments. And I, along with everyone else in the business, found that to be pretty damn cool.

But that seemingly ordinary day was disrupted by an article. The headline stood out clearly amid the online noise, as though it had been lobbed directly at me: "Growth Hacker Is the New VP [of] Marketing."

What?

I was a VP of marketing. I quite liked my job. I was good at it, too. Self-taught, self-made, I was, at twenty-five, helping to lead the efforts of a publicly traded company with 250 stores in twenty countries and more than $600 million in revenue.

But the writer, Andrew Chen, an influential technologist and entrepreneur, didn't care about any of that. According to him, my colleagues and I would soon be out of a job—someone was waiting in the wings to replace us.

> *The new job title of "Growth Hacker" is integrating itself into Silicon Valley's culture, emphasizing that coding and technical chops are now an essential part of being a great marketer. Growth hackers are a hybrid of marketer and coder, one who looks at the traditional question of "How do I get customers for my product?" and answers with A/B tests, landing pages, viral factor, email deliverability, and Open Graph....*
>
> *The entire marketing team is being disrupted. Rather than a VP of Marketing with a bunch of non-technical marketers reporting to them, instead growth hackers are engineers leading teams of engineers.[1]*

What the hell is a growth hacker? I thought. How could an engineer ever do my job?

But then I added up the combined valuation of the few companies Chen mentioned as case studies—companies that had barely existed a few years ago.

- **Dropbox**
- **Zynga**
- **Groupon**
- **Instagram**
- **Pinterest**

Now worth *billions and billions* of dollars.

As Micah Baldwin, founder of Graphicly and a start-up mentor at Techstars and 500 Startups, explains, "In the absence of big budgets, start-ups learned how to hack the system to build their companies."[2] Their hacking—which occurred right on my watch—had rethought marketing from the ground up, with none of the baggage or old assumptions. And now, their shortcuts, innovations, and backdoor solutions fly in the face of everything we've been taught.

We all want to do more with less. For marketers and entrepreneurs, that paradox is practically our job description. Well, in this book, we're going to look at how growth hackers have helped companies like Dropbox, Mailbox, Twitter, Pinterest, Facebook, Snapchat, Evernote, Instagram, Mint.com, AppSumo, and StumbleUpon do so much with essentially nothing.

What stunned me most about those companies was that none of them were built with any of the skills that traditional marketers like myself had always considered special, and most were built without the resources I'd long considered essential. I couldn't name the "marketer"— and definitely not the agency—responsible for their success because there wasn't one. Growth hacking had made "marketing" irrelevant, or at the very least it had completely rewritten its best practices.

Whether you're currently a marketing executive or a college grad about to enter the field—the first growth hackers have pioneered a new way. Some of their strategies are incredibly technical and complex. The strategies also change constantly; in fact, occasionally it might work only one time. This book is short because it sticks with the timeless parts. I also won't weigh you down with heavy concepts like "cohort analysis" and "viral coefficients."* Instead, we will focus on the mindset—it's far and away the most important part.

I start and end with my own experiences in this book, not because I am anyone special but because I think they illustrate a microcosm of the industry itself. The old way—where product development and marketing were two distinct and separate processes—has been replaced.

---

* But there is a glossary of important terms and concepts at the back of the book.

We all find ourselves in the same position: needing to do more with less and finding, increasingly, that the old strategies no longer generate results.

So in this book, I am going to take you through a new cycle, a much more fluid and iterative process. A growth hacker doesn't see marketing as something one does but rather as something one builds into the product itself. The product is then kick-started, shared, and optimized (with these steps repeated multiple times) on its way to massive and rapid growth. The chapters of this book follow that structure.

But first, let's make a clean break between the old and the new.

WHAT IS GROWTH HACKING?

> The end goal of every growth hacker is to build a *self-perpetuating marketing machine* that reaches millions by itself.
>
> —AARON GINN

There's no business like show business. Yet, when it comes right down to it, that's the industry every marketing team—no matter what business they're actually in—

pretends to be in when they're launching something new. Deep down, I think anyone marketing or launching fantasizes that they are premiering a blockbuster movie. And this illusion shapes and warps every marketing decision we make.

It feels good, but it's so very wrong.

Our first idea is a grand opening, a big launch, a press release, or major media coverage. We default to thinking we need an advertising budget. We want red carpet and celebrities. Most dangerously we assume we need to get as many customers as possible in a very short window of time—and if it doesn't work right away, we consider the whole thing a failure (which, of course, we cannot afford). Our delusion is that we should be *Transformers* and not *The Blair Witch Project*.

Needless to say, this is preposterous. Yet you and I have been taught, unquestionably, to follow it for years.

What's wrong with it? Well, for starters: *most movies fail.*

Despite the glamour and the history of movie marketing, even after investing millions—often more than the budget of the movie itself—studios regularly write off major releases as complete washes. And when they do succeed, no one has any idea why or which of the ingredients were responsible for it. As screenwriter William Goldman famously put it, *nobody knows anything*—even the people in charge. It's all a big gamble.

Which is fine, because their system is designed to absorb these losses. The hits pay for the mistakes many times over. But there is a big difference between them and everyone else in the world. You can't really afford for your start-up to fail; your friend has sunk everything into her new business; and I can't allow my book to flop. We don't have ten other projects coming down the pike. This is *it*.

It was only a matter of time before someone smart came along and said, "It doesn't have to be this way. The tools of the Internet and social media have made it possible to track, test, iterate, and improve marketing to the point where these enormous gambles are not only unnecessary, but insanely counterproductive."

That person was the first growth hacker.

A NEW WAY

If that old system is an outgrowth of one hundred years of marketing precedent—designed to fit the needs of twentieth-century corporations—then the new mindset began at the turn of the millennium. It began and evolved to meet the new needs of a new type of company—with its own kind of marketer.

Flash back to 1996, before Hotmail had launched as one of the first free web mail services and became an early example of a product to "go viral." As Adam Penenberg describes the meeting in *Viral Loop*, Hotmail's founders, Sabeer Bhatia and Jack Smith, sat across the table from Tim Draper, the famous venture capitalist. He told them that he thought the product—web-based e-mail—was great but wondered how they'd get the word out.

Bhatia's first instinct was that industrial marketing approach we've been talking about: "We'll put it up on billboards," he said. Draper nixed such an expensive approach for what would be a *free* product. So they kicked around more ideas. Radio ads? Same problem. What about sending an e-mail to everyone on the Internet? Draper suggested. That was an equally old mindset—spam doesn't work.

Then Draper happened accidentally on growth hacking. "Could you," he asked, "put a message at the bottom of everybody's screen?"

"Oh, come on, we don't want to do that!"

"But can you technically do it? . . . It can persist, right? You can put it on one message, and if he sends an e-mail to somebody else you can put it on that one, too, right?"

"Yeah, yeah," they replied.

"So put 'P.S.: I love you. Get your free e-mail at Hotmail' at the bottom."[3]

———

This little feature changed everything. It meant every e-mail that Hotmail's users sent would be an advertisement for the product. And that advertisement was effective not because it was cute or creative but because it showcased an amazing product that many people wanted and needed. Each user meant new users; each e-mail meant more e-mails and more happy customers. And most crucial, all this could be tracked and tweaked and improved to drive as many users as possible into the service.

You have to understand how revolutionary this was at the time. Consider that just a few years later, Pets.com would try to launch with a multicity television and outdoor advertising campaign that culminated in a $1.2-million Super Bowl commercial and an appearance at the Macy's Thanksgiving Day Parade. Or that Kozmo.com would blow through literally hundreds of millions of dollars with advertising campaigns featuring the Six Million Dollar Man before collapsing like Pets.com in the burst dot-com bubble.

But after adopting Draper's suggestion—which the

founders resisted for the first few months because it seemed so simple—growth was exponential: one million members within six months. Five weeks after that, membership had doubled again. By December 1997, with nearly ten million users, Hotmail was sold to Microsoft for $400 million. It took just thirty months from its launch for Hotmail to accumulate its thirty millionth user. And though it has now been renamed, Hotmail still exists, unlike the majority of its peers from that era.

This is the power of the new approach. A $400-million brand was launched and built with just a $300,000 investment—what a Hollywood studio or a Fortune 500 company might spend on a decent premiere party or single television commercial. Implemented and executed by people without the slightest bit of marketing experience.

And in case you think Hotmail was some fluke of the tech bubble, let me remind you that a few years later, Google launched Gmail—now the dominant free e-mail service—with essentially the same growth hacking strategies. First Google built a superior product. Then it built excitement by making it invite-only. And by steadily increasing the number of invites allowed to its existing user base, Gmail spread from person to person until it became the most popular, and in many ways the best, free e-mail service.

Enormous services launched from tiny but incredibly

explosive ideas. That's what we're going to study in this book.

THE RISE OF THE GROWTH HACKER

Since Hotmail, many other companies—particularly in the tech space—have begun to push and break through the limits of marketing. With a mind for data and a scrappy disregard for the "rules," they have pioneered a new model of marketing designed to utilize the many new tools that the Internet has made available: E-mail. Data. Social media. Bootstrapping.

Almost overnight, this breed has become the new rock stars of the Silicon Valley. You see them on the pages of *TechCrunch, Fast Company, Mashable, Inc., Entrepreneur,* and countless other publications. LinkedIn and Hacker News abound with job postings: Growth Hacker Needed.

Their job isn't to "do" marketing as I had always known it; it's to grow companies really fast—to take something from nothing and make it something enormous within an incredibly tight window. And it says something about what marketing has become that these are no longer considered synonymous tasks.

The term "growth hacker" has many different meanings

for different people, but I'll define it as I have come to understand it:

> *A growth hacker is someone who has thrown out the playbook of traditional marketing and replaced it with only what is testable, trackable, and scalable. Their tools are e-mails, pay-per-click ads, blogs, and platform APIs instead of commercials, publicity, and money. While their marketing brethren chase vague notions like "branding" and "mind share," growth hackers relentlessly pursue users and growth—and when they do it right, those users beget more users, who beget more users. They are the inventors, operators, and mechanics of their own self-sustaining and self-propagating growth machine that can take a start-up from nothing to something.*

But don't worry, I'm not going to belabor definitions in this book. What's important is we're all trying to grow our business, launch our website, sell tickets for our event, or fund our Kickstarter project. And the way we do it today is fundamentally different from how it used to be done.

Instead of launching products with multimillion-dollar marketing budgets, the growth hackers we will follow in this book began their work at start-ups with little to no resources. Forced to innovate and motivated to try new things, growth hackers like these have built some of these companies into billion-dollar brands. They did so not only outside the enormous edifice of the Hollywood-industrial-launch-complex but also *because* they ignored it and rejected its tactics. Instead of bludgeoning the public with ads or dominating the front page of newspapers to drive awareness, they used a scalpel, precise and targeted to a specific audience.

THE NEW MINDSET

Deep down, traditional marketers have always considered themselves artists. That's fine—it's an image I aspired to myself. It's a sentiment responsible for spectacular and moving work. But this sentiment is also responsible for some appalling ignorance and waste. One *Harvard Business Review* study found that 80 percent of marketers are unhappy with their ability to measure marketing return on investment (ROI). Not because the tools aren't good enough, but because they're *too* good, and marketers are seeing for the first time that their strategies are "often flawed and their spending is inefficient."[4]

Noah Kagan, a growth hacker at Facebook, the personal finance service Mint.com (which sold to Intuit for nearly $170 million), and the daily deal site AppSumo (which has more than eight hundred thousand users), explains it simply: "Marketing has always been about the same thing—who your customers are and where they are."[5]

What growth hackers do is focus on the "who" and "where" more scientifically, in a more measurable way. Whereas marketing was once brand-based, with growth hacking it becomes metric and ROI driven. Suddenly, finding customers and getting attention for your product are no longer guessing games. But this is more than just marketing with better metrics; this is not just "direct marketing" with a new name.

Growth hackers trace their roots back to programmers—and that's how they see themselves. They are data scientists meets design fiends meets marketers. They welcome this information, process it and utilize it differently, and see it as desperately needed clarity in a world that has been dominated by gut instincts and artistic preference for too long. But they also add a strong acumen for strategy, for thinking big picture, and for leveraging platforms, unappreciated assets, and new ideas.

Ultimately that's why this new approach is better suited to the future. With the collapse or crumbling of some behemoth industries and the rapid rise of start-ups, apps, and websites, marketing will need to get smaller—it will need to change its priorities. When you get right down to it, the real skill for marketers today isn't going to be helping some big, boring company grow 1 percent a year but creating a totally new brand from nothing using next-to-no resources. Whether that's a Kickstarter project you're trying to fund or a new app, the thinking is the same: how do you get, maintain, and multiply attention in a scalable and efficient way?

Thankfully, growth hacking isn't some proprietary technical process shrouded in secrecy. In fact, it has grown and developed in the course of very public conversations. There are no trade secrets to guard. Aaron Ginn, the growth hacker tasked with rapidly updating the technology behind Mitt Romney's presidential campaign and now director of growth at StumbleUpon, put it best: *growth hacking is more of a mindset than a tool kit.*

The good news: it's as simple as changing your mindset. (Or if you're just starting out in marketing, it means you've been spared the baggage of the old guard.) Growth hacking is not a 1-2-3 sequence but instead a fluid process.* Growth hacking at its core means putting aside the notion that marketing is a self-contained act that begins toward the end of a company's or a product's

---

* For anyone who is fascinated by this, I strongly suggest looking up John Boyd, the famous fighter pilot/strategist, and his concept of the OODA Loop.

development life cycle. It is, instead, a way of thinking and looking at your business.

The tools will vary from job to job—it's the mindset that will be the killer advantage, and I promise that when you finish reading this book, you will fully grasp the growth hacker's way of thinking. The chapters in this book are organized to guide you through the process of taking something from one user to a million and possibly to a hundred times that. I am compressing everything I've learned in the past two years studying, researching, and interviewing the world's best growth hackers.

I want to show you the growth hacker's way and why it is the future. How it's infiltrating the next generation of companies; how it's reshaping marketing, PR, and advertising from top to bottom; how even authors are using the principles in their book launches.

And that process starts far earlier than you think. The new marketing mindset begins not a few weeks before launch but, in fact, during the development and design phase. So we will begin there, with the most important marketing decision you will likely ever make.

GROWTH
HACKER
MARKETING

IT BEGINS WITH
PRODUCT MARKET FIT

Make something people want.

—PAUL GRAHAM

You know what the single worst marketing decision you can make is? Starting with a product nobody wants or nobody needs.

Yet for years, this was a scenario that marketers tolerated and accepted as part of the job. We all told ourselves that "you go to market with the product you have, not the one you want." And then we wondered why our strategies failed—and why those failures were so expensive.

What attracted me to growth hacking from the very start was that it rejects this obviously flawed approach outright. Growth hackers believe that products—even whole businesses and business models—can and should be changed until they are primed to generate explosive reactions from the first people who see them. In other words, the best marketing decision you can make is to have a product or business that fulfills a real and compelling need for a real and defined group of people—no matter how much tweaking and refining this takes.

Take Airbnb, a start-up now valued at some $10 billion. Today we know it as a site where, as cofounder Brian Chesky put it, "you can book space anywhere. It can be anything, and it really is anything from a tent to a castle."[6] But in 2007, the business started as a way for the founders to turn the living room of their loft apartment into a little bed-and-breakfast. The founders named it Air bedandbreakfast.com and put out air mattresses on their floor and offered free homemade breakfast to guests. But the founders wanted more.

Going back to the drawing board and hoping to capitalize on popular technology and design conferences, the founders repositioned the service as a networking alternative for attendees when hotels were booked up. This was clearly a better market, but the company sensed they could improve the idea further, so they pivoted slightly to target the type of traveler who didn't want to crash on couches or in hostels but was looking to avoid hotels. This did better still. Finally, based on feedback and usage patterns, they shortened the name to Airbnb and abandoned the breakfast and networking parts of the business, redefining the service as a place for people to rent or book any kind of lodging imaginable (from rooms to apartments to trains, boats, castles, penthouses, and private islands). This was explosive—to the tune of millions of bookings a year in locations all over the world.

Airbnb had a good idea in 2007, but the actual value proposition, if we're being honest, was a little mediocre. The founders could have spent all their time and energy trying to force the "let people crash on your floor and feed them breakfast" angle and creating a small business around it. Instead, they treated their product and service as something malleable and were able to change and improve it until they found its best iteration. They went from a good but fairly impractical idea to an explosive and practical idea, and then as a result, a billion-dollar valuation. This switch was undoubtedly the best marketing decision they ever could have made.

As a traditional marketer, I can think of precisely zero times when we went back to the drawing board after seeing a less-than-stellar response. It wasn't permitted. Our only move was to put more muscle behind bad products and companies.

It was a wake-up call to me to learn that Airbnb was by no means unique: Instagram started as a location-based social network called Burbn (which had an *optional* photo feature). It attracted a core group of users and more than

$500,000 in funding. And yet the founders realized that its users were flocking to only one part of the app—the photos and filters. They had a meeting, which one of the founders recounts like this: "We sat down and said, 'What are we going to work on next? How are we going to evolve this product into something millions of people will want to use? What is the one thing that makes this product unique and interesting?'"[7]

The service soon retooled to become Instagram as we know it: a mobile app for posting photos with filters. The result? One hundred thousand users within a week of relaunching. Within eighteen months, the founders sold Instagram to Facebook for $1 billion.

I know that seems simple, that the marketing lesson from Instragram is that they made a product that was just awesome. But that's good news for you—it means there's no secret sauce, and the second your product gets to be that awesome, you can see similar results. Just look at Snapchat, which essentially followed the same playbook by innovating in the mobile photo app space, blew up with young people, and skyrocketed to a $3.5-*billion*-dollar valuation with next-to-no marketing.

Some companies like Airbnb and Instragram spend a long time trying new iterations until they achieve what growth hackers call Product Market Fit (PMF); others find it right away. The end goal is the same, however, and it's to have the product and its customers in perfect sync with each other. Eric Ries, author of *The Lean Startup*, explains that the best way to get to Product Market Fit is by starting with a "minimum viable product" and improving it based on feedback—as opposed to what most of us do, which is to try to launch publicly with what we think is our final, perfected product.

Today, it is the marketer's job as much as anyone else's to make sure Product Market Fit happens. Your marketing efforts are wasted on a mediocre product—so don't tolerate mediocrity. OK?

But rather than waiting for it to happen magically or assuming that this is some other department's job, marketers need to contribute to this process. Isolating who your customers are, figuring out their needs, designing a product that will blow their minds—these are marketing decisions, not just development and design choices.

The imperative is clear: stop sitting on your hands and start getting them dirty. Optimizing a product to spread and be well received by customers, by the media, and by influencers is something that you, as a marketer or a growth hacker, are uniquely qualified to do. You are, in effect, the translator who helps bridge the producers and the consumers so they are in alignment.

And this is true whether you're making some physical gadget, designing a menu, or creating an app. Someone has to be the advocate for the potential market (customers), and the earlier their influence is felt in the process, the better.

Amazon has actually made this part of their basic procedures. Ian McAllister, general manager at Amazon, calls this approach "working backwards from the customer." For new initiatives, employees begin by creating an internal press release that announces this new potential project as though it was just finished. It's addressed to the customers—whoever they happen to be—and explains how this new offering solves their problems in an exciting or compelling way.[8]

If the press release cannot do that, the initiative is tweaked and tweaked and tweaked until it can. According to McAllister, Amazon encourages product managers to think like Oprah—that is, would she rapturously shout about this product if she were giving it away to her fans as a gift?

The exercise forces the team to focus on exactly what its potential new product is and what's special about it. I guarantee that someone with a mind that bends toward growth hacking put this policy into place.

No longer content to let the development happen as it happens, we can influence it with input, with rules and guidelines, and with feedback. The growth hacker helps with iterations, advises, and analyzes every facet of the business. In other words, Product Market Fit is a feeling backed with *data and information.*

HOW DO YOU GET PMF?

Because Product Market Fit can be overwhelming as a technical business concept, allow me to explain it by dropping the jargon and presenting an analogy. As it turns out, I was familiar with PMF long before I read Andrew Chen's article.

Much of the marketing I do is with authors and books. I've worked with dozens of bestsellers in the last five years—and, of course, I've also worked on many books that weren't successful. In my experience, the books that tend to flop upon release are those where the author goes into a cave for a year to write it, then hands it off to the publisher for release. They hope for a hit that rarely comes.

On the other hand, I have clients who blog extensively before publishing. They develop their book ideas based on the themes that they naturally gravitate toward but that also get the greatest response from readers. (One client sold a book proposal using a screenshot of Google queries to his site.) They test the ideas they're writing about in the book on their blog and when they speak in front of groups. They ask readers what they'd like to see in the book. They judge topic ideas by how many comments a given post generates, by how many Facebook "shares" an article gets. They put potential title and cover ideas up online to test and receive feedback. They look to see what hot topics other influential bloggers are riding and find ways of addressing them in their book.*

The latter achieves PMF; the former never does. One is growth hacking; the other, simply guessing.

One is easy for me to market. The other is often a lost cause. One needs only a small shove to get going. The other has a strong headwind every step of the way.

Amazon, for its part, has a couple of other easy suggestions for you if the advice "write a hypothetical press release" doesn't quite work for your situation. Their CTO, Werner Vogels, suggests trying to write an FAQ for this product you're developing. (That way you can address, in advance, potential user issues and questions.)[9] Or try to define the crucial parts of the user experience by making mockups of pages, writing hypothetical case studies so you can actually start to see what it would look like and who it would work for and how. Finally, try writing the user manual, which as Werner explains usually has three parts: concepts, how-to, and reference. (Defining these means you understand your idea in and out from the customers per-

---

* This paperback began as a much shorter eBook and before that a successful article.

spective. Also, he says, if you have more than one type of user then write multiple manuals.)

I love those ideas. They might feel like homework, but they force you to imagine your product from someone's perspective other than your own. That's the best way to get to PMF—because ultimately this isn't about you; it's about the people you're trying to turn into customers.

Perhaps you'll get to PMF with one aha moment like Instagram, or it may be incremental 1 percent improvements. As Marc Andreessen—the entrepreneur behind Netscape, Opsware, and Ning who, in addition to running a major venture capital fund, happens to be on the board of directors for Facebook, eBay, and HP—explains it, companies need to "do whatever is required to get to product/market fit. Including changing out people, rewriting your product, moving into a different market, telling customers no when you don't want to, telling customers yes when you don't want to, raising that fourth round of highly dilutive venture capital—whatever is required."[10]

In other words: everything is now on the table.

OPEN UP TO FEEDBACK

Part of this new approach is having the humility to accept that marketers are not necessarily the most critical members of the team. It's true. Sometimes the best thing marketers can do is to not let people get distracted by "marketing" for a minute. Sometimes the outward-facing part of the job is exactly the least important part.

Take Evernote, a start-up that offers productivity and organization software, which made the companywide decision to delay spending even a penny on marketing for the first several years of its growth. As Evernote's founder, Phil Libin, told a group of entrepreneurs in a now-classic talk, "People [who are] thinking about things other than making the best product, never make the best product." So Evernote took "marketing" off the table and instead poured that budget into product development. This undoubtedly slowed brand building at first—but it paid off. Why? Because Evernote is far and away the most superior productivity and note-taking application on the planet. Today, it practically markets itself.

Perhaps this is what you need to do. I know you're probably reading this book looking for some immediate tips you can put into action—places you can deploy your budget or resources. But let's think outside the box— outside the budget—and consider whether improving your product might be the best strategy.

That's not to say you shouldn't do anything at all. Evernote still came up with a bunch of clever tricks to get people to see its products while marketing was on their strategic back burner. After hearing customers complain that their bosses were suspicious of employees using their laptops in meetings, the Evernote team produced stickers that said, "I'm not being rude. I'm taking notes in Evernote." Thus, their most loyal customers were turning into billboards that went from meeting to meeting.

Once we stop thinking of the products we market as static—that our job as marketers is to simply work with what we've got instead of *working on* and *improving* what we've got—the whole game changes. Now we are not helpless, repeatedly pitching a product to reporters and users that is not resonating. Instead, we use this information to improve the product, with the idea of ultimately refining our idea into something that can in many ways sell itself.

The race has changed. The prize and spoils no longer go to the person who makes it to market first. They go to the person who *makes it to Product Market Fit first*. Because once you get there, your marketing efforts become like a spark applied to a bed of kindling soaked in kerosene. The old way? It's striking a match . . . and hoping it starts a fire somewhere.

The point is: marketing as we know it is a waste of time without PMF.

Of course, there are many tools to help get you there. From Google to Optimizely to KISSmetrics, there are great services that allow you to see what your users are actually doing and responding to on your site. This insight will get you closer to a fit than gut instincts ever will.

But the most effective method is simply the Socratic method. We must simply and repeatedly question every assumption. Who is this product for? Why would they use it? Why do *I* use it?

Ask your customers questions, too: What is it that brought you to this product? What is holding you back from referring other people to it? What's missing? What's golden? Don't ask random people or your friends—be scientific about it. Use tools like SurveyMonkey, Wufoo, Qualaroo, or even Google Docs, which make it very easy to offer surveys to some or all of your customers.

For the first time we can ask these questions because we intend to *do* something about it. No more privately complaining to friends, coworkers, and spouses that we're stuck with a product nobody wants.

Not to say that you must use *all* the data that comes back, but you should have it. The black-box approach is no longer necessary. Change is possible—which means you need to make yourself available and open to it.

Product Market Fit is not some mythical status that happens accidentally. Companies work for it; they crawl toward it. They're ready to throw out weeks or months of work because the evidence supports that decision. The services as their customers know them now are fundamentally different from what they were at launch—before they had Product Market Fit.

But once these companies get PMF, they don't just wait and hope that success will come along on its own. The next step is to bring the customers in.

FINDING YOUR GROWTH HACK

To be successful and grow your business and revenues, you must match the way you market your products with the way your prospects learn about and shop for your products.

—BRIAN HALLIGAN, FOUNDER OF HUBSPOT

With growth hacking, we begin by testing until we can be confident we have a product worth marketing. Only then do we chase the big bang that kick-starts our growth engine. Without this jump, even the best-designed products and greatest ideas go nowhere.

For instance, many people don't know that the late Aaron Swartz, the genius hacker responsible for reddit, also invented two other services. In 1999, he started a collaborative encyclopedia before *Wikipedia*. He started another site called Watchdog.net, which was very similar to the wildly popular Change.org. Both were clearly fantastic ideas, predating the actual services we all use today.

But Aaron's services never attracted an initial group of users and thus failed.

As Larissa MacFarquhar wrote in her *New Yorker* profile of him, "[Aaron] had previously believed that if you came up with a great idea people would use it. But he realized now that you couldn't expect people to come to you; you had to pull them in."[11]

The growth hacker's job—like we marketers have always done—is to do that pulling.

But how? Certainly not with the expensive or inefficient methods of old. As a loyal company man at American Apparel, I hate to say this, but just buying some T-shirts with your company name on them is not going to do it. It might be fun, it might make you feel special, but that's not how you make your company the next big thing, OK?

At the same time, with Product Market Fit, we don't need to hit the front page of the *New York Times* to announce our launch. We need only to hit the *New York Times* of *our* scene. We're trying to hit a few hundred or a thousand key people—not millions. That's a relief, right? Better still, it actually works.

In other words, launching does not need to be an enormous campaign we're expected (too often) to produce out of thin air so much as an initial boost or a shot in the arm. Not a blowout grand opening, but a strategic opening or a stunt that catches the attention of our core audience.

So, yes, like the old model, growth hacking still requires pulling your customers in. Except you seek to do it in a cheap, effective, and usually unique and new way. Whereas all traditional marketing starts the same way—with a news story or an advertising campaign—start-ups can launch in a multitude of ways.

Take Dropbox. Today it has more than three hundred million users, but when the file-sharing service began, it was not even open to the public. New users had to sign up to a waiting list to be invited to join. In an effort to drive these sign-ups, the founders crafted a fun demo video that walked potential users through the service.

They didn't hire some production company to produce an expensive or elaborate video that they jammed down people's throats through widespread ads. They made the video themselves, and they made the right one for the right place. Knowing the outlets where they intended to post the video (Digg, Slashdot, and reddit), they filled it with all sorts of jokes, allusions, and references that those communities would eat up.

As a result, this homemade video was enormously popular with these potential users. It immediately made the respective front pages, it drove hundreds of thousands of new visitors to the special page Dropbox had set up for this purpose (GetDropbox.com), and the waiting list went from five thousand users to seventy-five thousand users nearly overnight. It was all trackable, all visible, and highly effective.

This was all Dropbox really needed. After sending a highly targeted burst of traffic to the site, the team didn't turn around and say, "Okay, how can we get on the news for this tonight?" They didn't need it. Within just a short amount of time, those initial seventy-five thousand users became nearly four million, which, in turn, grew to the more than three hundred million people they have today.

A few years later, the e-mail app Mailbox launched with a similar strategy. An incredibly compelling—albeit a tad more professional—demo video racked up one hundred thousand views in less than four hours. This one-minute video, combined with a very cool interface that showed users how many other users were in front of them on the app's waiting list, created a spectacle that drove an enormous amount of social chatter and blog attention. Within six weeks, Mailbox had a million users signed up and eagerly waiting for the service.

Would it work again for another company? Maybe; or maybe that growth hack is now played out. The point is, you've got to find something new and exciting and channel that energy toward exploding on the market with your product.

Also, let me get one potential objection out of the way right now: this is not just about finding your *first* customers. Established brands and companies can use the same techniques to pull in more customers. Growth is growth.

Look at eBay, which in 2012 partnered with Gogo—the inflight wifi provider—to provide free access to eBay .com for customers on Delta and Virgin America flights. (That is, the wifi service still costs money but anyone with a laptop can get on for free to browse eBay.) What is eBay doing with this move? Well, they're getting a crack at hundreds of thousands of potential customers (bored and stuck ones at that) via someone else's platform—proving that even original tech-bubble companies can still growth hack.

And the most important lesson in this particular play? Because it's digital and platform driven, eBay can easily track the revenues and traffic sent to their site from Gogo.* To decide whether they should continue, cancel, or expand to other in-flight wifi carriers, all eBay will need to do is compare the cost of their deal with

---

* Meanwhile the *New York Times* runs what is likely very expensive "branded content" on JetBlue's in-flight TV screens for what I am sure are completely untraceable results. That is *not* growth hacking. Neither are ads in the in-flight magazine.

Gogo against the revenues brought in by those users. It's brilliant.

It's no wonder that a bunch of other e-commerce retailers are following suit.

NOT ALL PEOPLE—THE *RIGHT* PEOPLE

The old mindset says go out and get everyone you conceivably can. This pressure comes from our clients, and many marketers have internalized these self-destructively ambitious goals. I know the feeling: *I want to be everywhere. I want millions of video views. I want to become a trending Twitter topic.* They try to go everywhere and end up going nowhere.

What's the point? Most of those people never become your customers.

Growth hackers resist this temptation (or, more appropriate, this delusion). They opt, deliberately, to attract only the early adopters who make or break new tech services and seek to do it as cheaply as possible. In fact, part of the reason the scrappy start-ups, services, and apps in this book might not always be well-known or topics of daily conversation is because their founders have focused their energies on product development with an eye toward growth—they're now millions of members strong without any superfluous "buzz." They got to mass market by ignoring the urge to appeal to the mass market, at least to start with.

This means that our outward-facing marketing and PR efforts are needed simply to reach out to and capture, at the beginning, a group of highly interested, loyal, and fanatical users. Then we grow with and because of them.

If they are geeks, they are at *TechCrunch* or Hacker News or reddit or attending a handful of conferences every year.

If they are fashionistas, they are regularly checking a handful of fashion blogs like Lookbook.nu or Hypebeast.

If they are _____, like you and your founders are, they are reading and doing the same things you do every day.

Catch their attention and pull them in. It's as simple as that.

Uber, a car service start-up founded by Travis Kalanick and Garrett Camp, has been giving out free rides during Austin's SXSW conference for several years. During a single week, thousands of potential Uber customers— tech-obsessed, high-income young adults who cannot find a cab—are motivated to try out this service. One year Uber offered free rides. Another year, it offered BBQ delivery. Instead of spending millions on advertising or countless resources trying to reach these potential users in their respective cities, Uber just waited for the one week a year when they were all in one place and did something special. And Uber did this because a few years earlier they'd watched Twitter take SXSW by storm with a similar collaboration with the conference.

This is thinking like a growth hacker—it's how you get the most bang for your buck and how you get it from the *right* people.

(A very common question: Where do I find the right people? If this isn't immediately obvious to you, then you don't know your own industry well enough to even consider launching a product yet. Period.)

To kick off and reach your first group of users, you have many options:

1. You can reach out to the sites you know your potential customers read with a pitch e-mail: "This is who we are, this is what we're doing, and this is why you should write about us."*
2. You can upload a post to Hacker News, Quora, or reddit yourself.

---

* As I wrote in my first book, *Trust Me, I'm Lying*, the economics of the media have fundamentally changed. Instead of being an environment of scarcity, like a newspaper, where the editors can publish only a limited amount of stories, the inventory online is infinite. Meaning: bloggers are happy to write about anything that will appeal to their audience.

3.   You can start writing blog posts about popular topics that get traffic and indirectly pimp your product.

4.   You can use the Kickstarter platform for exposure and bribe your first users with cool prizes (and get some online chatter at the same time).

5.   You can use a service like Help a Reporter Out (www.helpareporter.com) to find reporters who are *looking* for people to include in stories they are already writing about your space.

6.   You can find your potential customers one by one and invite them to your service for free or with some special incentive (that's how small we're talking).

Getting on one or two of these outlets is as simple as sending a quick e-mail—after all, if your product really is specially designed for these people, they *want* to feature it.

The point is: do whatever it takes to pull in a small contingent of initial users from your particular space.

Sometimes "stunts" are a great way to do that. It's often about exploiting systems or platforms that others have not yet fully appreciated.

Patrick Vlaskovits, who was part of the initial

conversation that the term "growth hacker" came out of, put it well: "The more innovative your product is, the more likely you will have to find new and novel ways to get at your customers."[12]

For example:

1. You can create the aura of exclusivity with an invite-only feature (as Mailbox did).
2. You can create hundreds of fake profiles to make your service look more popular and active than it actually is—nothing draws a crowd like a crowd (as reddit did in its early days).
3. You can target a single service or platform and cater to it exclusively—essentially piggybacking off or even stealing someone else's growth (as PayPal did with eBay).
4. You can launch for just a small group of people, own that market, and then move from host to host until your product spreads like a virus (which is what Facebook did by starting in colleges—first at Harvard—before taking on the rest of the population).
5. You can host cool events and drive your first users through the system manually (as Myspace, Yelp, and Udemy all did).

6. You can absolutely dominate the App Store because your product provides totally new features that everyone is dying for (which is what Instagram did—twenty-five thousand downloads on its first day—and later Snapchat).

7. You can bring on influential advisors and investors for their valuable audience and fame rather than their money (as About.me and Trippy did—a move that many start-ups have emulated).

8. You can set up a special sub-domain on your e-commerce site where a percentage of every purchase users make goes to a charity of their choice (which is what Amazon did with Smile.Amazon.com this year to great success, proving that even a successful company can find little growth hacks).

9. You can try to name a Planned Parenthood clinic after your client or pay D-list celebrities to say offensive things about themselves to get all sorts of publicity that promotes your book (OK, those stunts were mine).

All of these types of outreach are done with a very specific mindset, with a very specific goal. We are not "spreading the word"; we're not throwing up a billboard in Times Square and hoping in six months someone will spot our product in a grocery store and decide to pick it up. Instead, we are intensely focused on driving an initial set of new user sign-ups and customers, right now.

It doesn't matter how many people know about you or how they find out about you. It matters how many sign up. If handing out flyers on the street corner accomplishes that, then consider it growth hacking.

Each one of the previously mentioned strategies was, in its own way, a bit like a Trojan horse. By doing one thing, something that often didn't feel like marketing, a company was able to get access to users that it was then able to convert into customers, clients, or sign-ups. So, what's your Trojan horse going to be?

LET'S GET TECHNICAL

The movie marketing paradigm says throw an expensive premiere and *hope* that translates into ticket sales come opening weekend. A growth hacker says, "Hey, it's the twenty-first century, and we can be a lot more technical about how we acquire and capture new customers."

The start-up world is full of companies taking clever

hacks to drive their first set of customers into their sales funnel. The necessity of that jolt—needing to get it any way they can—has made start-ups very creative.

Let's look at Airbnb again. The company's most effective marketing tactic (besides making a great product) would never have been conceived or attempted by a pure marketing team. Instead, the engineers coded a set of tools that made it possible for every member to seamlessly cross-post his or her Airbnb listing on craigslist (because craigslist does not technically "allow" this, it was a fairly ingenious work-around). As a result, Airbnb—a tiny site—suddenly had free distribution on one of the most popular websites in the world.

As Andrew Chen wrote in a case study of this tactic:

> *Let's be honest, a traditional marketer would not even be close to imagining the integration above—there's too many technical details needed for it to happen. As a result, it could only have come out of the mind of an engineer tasked with the problem of acquiring more users from Craigslist.[13]*

I don't think a direct marketer—with their proclivities for cheap advertisements or mail—would have thought of that either. This is a totally different approach. In this case, it's half strategy, half engineering. The combination is going to be different in every situation, but the point is that it's always outside-the-box, even outside-the-budget.

Today, as a marketer, our task isn't necessarily to "build a brand" or even to maintain a preexisting one. We're better off building an army of immensely loyal and passionate users. Which is easier to track, define, and grow? Which of these is real, and which is simply an idea? And when you get that right—a brand will come naturally.

As Sean Ellis, one of the first growth hackers—he coined the term with Patrick Vlaskovits—puts it: "Focusing on customer acquisition over 'awareness' takes discipline.... At a certain scale, awareness/brand building makes sense. But for the first year or two it's a total waste of money."[14]

The most insidious part of the traditional marketing model is that "big blowout launch" mythology. Of course, equally seductive is the "build it and they will come" assumption that too many people associate with the Web. Both are too simple and rarely effective.

Remember what Aaron Swartz realized. Users have to be pulled in. A good idea is not enough. Your customers, in fact, have to be "acquired." But the way to do that isn't with a bombardment. It's with a targeted offensive in the *right* places aimed at the *right* people.

Your start-up is designed to be a growth engine—and at some point early on, that engine has to be kick-started. The good news is that we have to do that only once. Because the next step isn't about getting more attention or publicity. The endless promotional cycle of traditional marketing is not our destiny. Because once we bring our first customers in, our next move is to set about turning them into an army.

STEP 3

TURN 1 INTO 2 AND
2 INTO 4—GOING VIRAL

Virality isn't luck. It's not magic. And it's not random. There's a science behind why people talk and share. A recipe. A formula, even.

—JONAH BERGER

You've heard it in a million meetings. And clients are so flip about it: "We want to go viral. Make people share this online."

Everyone wants it. As though massive viral sharing is as simple as asking for it. All I know is that I cringe each time I hear a client make that assumption.

The growth hacker has a response: Well, why should customers do that? Have you actually made it easy for them to spread your product? Is the product even worth talking about?

It's stunning how rarely people venture to answer this

question, myself included. They assume that "going viral"—benefiting from a rapid, contagious, person-to-person spread—is something that can magically happen to any product. But virality is not some accident.

Even when it seems accidental, it really isn't. Take something like the Holstee Manifesto, an inspiring mission statement about following your dreams and living your passion, written by a small apparel company in Brooklyn. Because it was so much more than self-promotion, the short video graphic the owners designed went on to be seen more than sixty million times and was translated into dozens of languages.

Did the founders expect it to go viral and launch their company in front of many new customers? No, but because it was inspiring, moving, directed at a specific audience, and concise, it had a far better chance of doing so than the countless boring and meaningless mission statements written by other companies each and every day.

Only a specific type of product or business or piece of content will go viral—it not only has to be worth spreading, it has to provoke a desire in people to spread it. Until you have accomplished that, or until your client is doing something truly remarkable, it just isn't going to happen.

Look, virality at its core is asking someone to spend their social capital recommending or linking or posting about you for *free*. You're saying: Post about me on Facebook. Tell your friends to watch my video. Invite your business contacts to use this service. The best way to get people to do this enormous favor for you? Make it seem like it isn't a favor. Make it the kind of thing that is worth spreading and, of course, conducive to spreading.

It goes without saying why viral spread is critical to the growth hacker approach. Once you have decided that you will not be paying to get in front of every potential customer (via paid advertisements or publicity), then you've accepted you must reach them some other way. That means you're relying on your users themselves to spread the word.

The crucial difference is that a growth hacker understands that this can't be left to chance; we can't wait and be pleasantly surprised like Holstee. Virality isn't something that comes *after* the fact. Instead, the product must be inherently worth sharing—and then on top of that, you must facilitate and encourage the spreading you'd like to see by adding tools and campaigns that enable virality.

One of the simplest and most straightforward examples of this is Groupon and LivingSocial, the daily deal pioneers. Each and every deal on these sites—which at the time of launch felt a lot more exciting than they do now—is accompanied by an additional offer. For Groupon, it's

"Refer a friend" and you get ten dollars when your friend makes his or her first purchase. For LivingSocial, it says, "Get this deal for free": if you buy the deal and recommend it to three friends who buy it via a special link, it's *free* for you. No matter how much the deal costs.

To make that clear: you should not just encourage sharing but create powerful incentives to do so. If your product isn't doing that right now, why would anyone share it? But if you do it right, people will advertise your product and feel like they are the ones getting something out of it!

I would feel bad if I didn't *share* my favorite story about incentives here. There is a service called DistroKid, which helps musicians get their songs listed on Spotify, iTunes, and Amazon. They rolled out a feature that gave the product away to users for free *if* they referred five friends who signed up.

Well, it turned out that a percentage of users were cheating—signing up five bogus accounts to get their membership comped. You'd think this could be a justification for shutting the program down or making it more stringent. In fact, the founder—taking a cue from a recent news story where a police officer *bought* groceries for a woman caught shoplifting—responded by creating a Scholarship. If you get caught taking advantage of the referral program, the system offers you two options: pay or accept a free membership on the house.[15]

How cool is that? This was a great PR move that got the company all sorts of attention, it kept the referral program in space, and, I'm sure, it converted those originally duplicitous users into hard-core evangelists for the product.

I hope it's clear how drastically different these approaches are from throwing some "Like this on Facebook" or "Post this on Twitter" buttons on the bottom of a blog post and expecting it to suddenly spread. Think about how much less Groupon, LivingSocial, and DistroKid had to spend on advertising because every offer had advertising built into it—they were not only paying their users to do it for them but also encouraging the new users to do the same thing.

PUBLIC-ITY

Jonah Berger, a social scientist well-known for his studies of virality, explains that publicness is one of the most crucial factors in driving something's spread. As he writes in his book *Contagious*, "Making things more observable makes them easier to imitate, which makes them more likely to become popular. . . . We need to design products and initiatives that advertise themselves and create behavioral residue that sticks around even after people have bought the product or espoused the idea."[16]

This is why many start-ups owe their now-massive user bases to thoughtful integration with big platforms.

Since the average Facebook user has more than 150 friends, it's incredibly powerful if they cross-post their Twitter posts on Facebook, say, or syndicate their Instagram photos.

Without question the massive growth and spread of Spotify, a music-streaming service launched in the United States in 2011, was largely driven by its integration into Facebook. How many of us saw that our friends were listening to it and thought, "Hey, maybe I should try it, too"?

Now, Spotify had a secret weapon in the fact that Sean Parker was an investor in both Spotify and Facebook and was able to get a sweetheart deal. Most of us don't have that kind of juice. But that doesn't mean we can't make our products more public and get free advertising out of it. We can use other people's networks to our advantage.

Dropbox, for instance, offered its customers a 150-megabyte storage bonus if they linked their Dropbox account to their Facebook or Twitter account.

Think of Hotmail, whose early attempts at growth hacking we looked at earlier. They turned every e-mail its users sent into a pitch to new customers. Think of Apple and BlackBerry, which turned their devices into advertising engines by adding "Sent from my iPhone" or "Sent from my BlackBerry" to every message sent.

Apple has been particularly forward-thinking in the art of crafting publicness into their product and marketing strategy. First off, with the launch of the iPod they made the crucial decision to make its headphones white instead of black. What many thought was just a minor aesthetic choice actually turned the millions of people who've bought devices from Apple into walking advertisements. And have you ever noticed what else comes inside the boxes of most Apple products? Apple stickers. Who knows how many the company has given out over the years this way—likely hundreds of millions at this point—many of which are now permanently stuck on walls, car bumpers, and devices (including those of ashamed PC owners) all over the world.

Now start-ups are following this lead. Mailbox, an in-box organizer, adds a "Sent from Mailbox" line to the end of its users' e-mails. When I filed my taxes this year with TurboTax, it asked me if I wanted to send out a prewritten tweet that said I'd gotten a refund by using its service. When I bought my first Bitcoin through Coinbase .com a few months ago, the checkout process prompted me to tweet "I just bought 1 Bitcoin @Coinbase! https:// coinbase.com." Though it seems to me that they could have easily coded a solution so the message included the price at which I'd bought it, which would have had the effect of advertising the rising value of the currency as well. Finally, my Dropcam makes it incredibly easy to publicly share clips that my camera makes—and actively suggests I do so. You'd think that there wouldn't be much benefit to do this when customers like me use them for security cameras, but when I caught my pet dachshund howling like a wolf one day when I wasn't home (having *never* seen a hint of this behavior in seven years), you can bet I shared the clip on Facebook and e-mail.

However companies decide to do it, it is all free branding—and that's immensely powerful.*

Remember, a growth hacker doesn't think branding is worthless, just that it's not worth the premium that traditional marketers pay for it. A growth hacker isn't going to try to create brand awareness by buying product placement on national television or by paying a celebrity to be associated with his or her product. Instead, a growth hacker will look for ways to get this social currency for free. They're looking to make the use of their product inherently public and to drive that branding through thousands of small user actions.

---

* Though I do think that Snapchat—whose private, disappearing texts are inherently *not* public—is an interesting counterexample. The service is very viral, but it isn't public. In fact, the brand is so cool precisely because it is private, hidden, and ephemeral. Its controversiality is what drives the word of mouth.

It's more meaningful this way, anyway, isn't it? To have a brand built through the voices and presence of your customers instead of through expensive commercials or from sponsoring golf tournaments?

GROWTH HACKING YOUR VIRALITY

Dropbox's founders, after pulling in their first set of users with their awesome demo video and social media strategy, had a choice. They could try to continue growing with the same tactics—more videos, more social media—or they could use advertising to boost their brand, because it was the conventional marketing wisdom. They tried the latter only to find that it cost between $233 and $388 in ad spend for every paying subscriber they brought in.[17] After more than fourteen months of struggling to find a growth engine, the Dropbox team had what they call their epiphany. Using an idea brought on by talks with the famous growth hacker Sean Ellis, Dropbox built one of the most effective and most viral referral programs of the start-up world.

It was as simple as placing a little "Get free space" button on the front page of the service. The offer was that users would get five hundred megabytes of free space for every friend they invited and got to sign up. Almost immediately, sign-ups increased by roughly 60 percent and stayed at that level for months. With more than 2.8 million direct invites a month because of the program, it's not hard to see why.

And remember, the alternative was paying upwards of $400 per person via advertising. You and I might not have studied math or computer science in school, but we can do the math there. Referrals versus paid advertising is the kind of A/B test whose results are obvious to everyone. Referrals win. And today, 35 percent of Dropbox's customers come to it via referral.

All of which is to say a simple truth that we try to deny too often: if you want to go viral, it must be baked into your product. There must be a reason to share it *and* the means to do so.

This is not easy. But once you begin to look at the world this way you can start to spot the opportunities. You'll understand that you can't just make a YouTube video about whatever you want and expect it to get ten million views. There has to be a compelling reason for a community to take hold of it and pass it around. You can't just expect your users to become evangelists of your product—you've got to provide the incentives and the platform for them to do so.

Virality is not an accident. It is *engineered*.

But we don't simply set up viral features and hope they work. Keeping our growth engine going is a step unto itself. We must dive deeply into the analytics available to us and refine, refine, refine until we get maximum results.

STEP 4

CLOSE THE LOOP: RETENTION AND OPTIMIZATION

> You need the kind of objectivity that makes you forget everything you've heard, clear the table, and do a factual study like a scientist would.
>
> —STEVE WOZNIAK

If the growth hacking process begins with something I would have previously considered to be outside the marketer's domain (product development), then I suppose it is only natural that it conclude with another.

The traditional marketer's job, as I learned in my time in fashion and publishing, is to get the leads—to bring in potential customers. It's someone else's job to figure out what to do with them.

But does that really make sense anymore?

First off, in a small company, there *is* no one else. Your job is not just to bring in potential customers but to create lifelong users. And, as it turns out, dedicated and happy users are marketing tools in and of themselves.

What's the point of driving a bunch of new customers through marketing channels if they immediately leak out through a hole in the bottom? What's the use of building up a certain perception of your product in the media and via marketing if the moment people try it they find out the hype isn't true?

Marketing doesn't have to be this Sisyphean job of driving people through the door or to a website. Today, analytics make it clear whether new users from your marketing initiatives actually stick. It's called "conversion rate." Know what it is and use it!

In its early days, Twitter experienced this exact issue. And its marketing team was wise enough to realize that the company's best marketing move had nothing to do with attracting more customers. Even though they could have bought ads, sent out e-mails, gotten more PR—that is, marketed—it wasn't what they needed. They needed to make the prospective users they were already getting *stick*.

Because the service was the subject of a lot of buzz online and in the media, new users were signing up for Twitter in droves. Yet most of them created an account and never really used it. That's where a growth hacker named Josh Elman came in. Poring over the stats, he and his team of twenty-five growth hackers (crazy, right?)

noticed that when users manually selected five to ten accounts to "follow" or "friend" on the first day, the user was significantly more likely to stick around.

As Elman explained it to me:

> *When I first joined the company, the suggested user list had 20 random people who were default selected to follow. Given this data insight, we reset the new user flow to encourage people to follow their first ~10 people and offer them a lot of choices, but no default selection. Then we later built a feature that continually suggested new users to follow on the sidebar of the website. These two changes helped people get started following, and more importantly understand that following was important to get the most out of Twitter. So over time more people did just this and became more and more likely to be retained.*[18]

This innovation has been responsible for millions of happy users, not just on Twitter but other social networks as well. For example, Pinterest, the popular design and inspiration community, has new users automatically follow a selection of high-quality Pinterest users. Anyone who joins is therefore much more likely to see compelling, attractive content right off the bat. It also gives users a great place to start rather than *hoping* they figure it out on their own.

I know this doesn't seem like marketing—it is quite literally a product/feature development decision. But if it drives better user adoption and makes users more engaged, it is. (Remember, if you've built in viral features, the more your users stick, the more it will spread.) These moves grew Twitter, and they grew Pinterest. Who could argue then that it *wasn't* great marketing?

Now every company is going to have their own metrics and definitions of what this is. Facebook's growth hackers saw that users who added seven friends in ten days were the most engaged and active—so that's what they designed features and campaigns to drive. At Zynga, it was all about D1 users—that is, users who came back after the first day. At Dropbox, it was dragging at least one file into your Dropbox folder—not just creating an account.[19]

Remember: metrics are somewhat relative depending on what you are trying to accomplish. Figure out what your most important metric for growth is and focus on that. Don't listen to or judge yourself on other people.

A great example of a company that didn't do that was Groupon. After the media pegged them as one of the fastest growing companies of all time, it looked like they became obsessed with growth because it was the simplest yardstick—not because it was the most important.

Growth hackers refer to such metrics as "vanity metrics." By way of analogy, what if Disneyland *predominately* measured itself with the raw number of park visitors each day? They would soon go astray—not just because the experience inside the park was being neglected but because the simple numbers like "total visitors" can be easily influenced by things like discounts, promotions, and outside events. Increases in park attendance are great . . . but can mask other problems. What matters is *happy* customers.

In Groupon's case, the service may have been posting superficially impressive stats, but in reality the public was getting increasingly fatigued with their products. Had Groupon been monitoring the customer experience more holistically, I bet they would have been able to see that all this growth was coming at an incredibly high cost. They were alienating their core users, who were abandoning the service—known as "churn"—even as new users joined.

On the other hand, Airbnb invested heavily in an expensive program that a lot of growth hackers doubted at first. In 2011, in an effort to improve the site's aesthetic appeal and attract higher-end customers, Airbnb began offering *free* professional photography for its listings. If you listed your house on the service, they'd send a pro over to taking amazing photos that made your house look irresistible. Why? Because, as they put it, "Taking crisp, well-lit and composed photographs that accurately convey the look and feel of the space is the most difficult part of creating a listing, so we make it easy."[20]

Though this approach is untraditional, you can see how this checks off so many growth hacking objectives. It increases the conversion rate, increases the price a listing can charge, draws members deeper into the community, weeds out potentially risky or negative listings, teaches users how to use the product better, makes them rave about the product, and just as a bonus, it got a bunch of positive publicity about it. Now tens of thousands of Airbnb listings on nearly every continent have been verified and improved by their team of freelance photographers.

This probably didn't seem like a marketing decision at the time. The person who suggested it was probably just thinking of a way to make the site better (or as they put it, make a difficult part of their process easier). Yes, there was an expense involved, but it was almost certainly a better bargain than a billboard ever would be, and the benefits will continue to accrue for it indefinitely. *That* kind of thinking is growth at its finest. No matter what business you're in, you can apply that to what you do and grow because of it.

ALWAYS BE TWEAKING

At the end of the day, we are all just trying to grow our businesses. What growth hackers have mastered is the ability to grow and expand their businesses without having to chase down new customers. At the end of the day, isn't this a lot easier and cheaper? Why not optimize internally instead of constantly chasing lead generation? They add up to the same thing: better and more profitable customers.

Aaron Ginn explained to me that even the best growth hacker cannot "grow a broken product."[21] Just because you've achieved Product Market Fit doesn't mean that your idea is flawless, that there aren't huge areas that still need to be tweaked and improved.

Sean Beausoleil, the engineering lead at Mailbox, put it more bluntly in an interview with *ReadWrite*: "Whatever your current state is, it can be better."[22] Growth hackers know this, and that is why they are trying new iterations constantly.

There is another simple Twitter growth hacking story that I like, by way of Andy Johns, a growth hacker there who also worked on growth at Facebook and Quora.[23] His team noticed that the antiquated system that Twitter used to send e-mails to its users was so bad that it often took the company three whole days to hit their entire list. Because of that, Twitter would usually send only one e-mail per customer per month. The growth team set aside some programmers to fix this and now, Twitter sends all sorts of highly effective (and automated) reminders, alerts, and notifications that have increased engagement and user recommendations. Even tweaking internal systems and procedures can have marketing implications.

Perhaps the front page of your site doesn't convert users as well as it should. Perhaps you're not generating enough e-mail addresses, or users make it 99 percent of the way through your shopping cart and then too many of them quit at the last second. Perhaps it takes too long for your social media team to get things posted or for new products to be rolled out onto the retail floor of your shop. Everything can be improved. The reality is that your product is probably broken in at least one way. A growth hacker uses all available information to figure out where those problems are and then *does something about them* as soon as possible.

This concept might not seem controversial, but it is. We all remember Myspace, which was awesome when it launched. But the product stopped improving. Its login process was infamous—it required users to click several different pages just to access their accounts—an annoying tactic Myspace employed out of greed to generate more advertising. The result was that users started to leave. Facebook's relentless pursuit of perfection and user experience stole Myspace's customers—just as Myspace had stolen then from Friendster. Don't be Myspace!

The role of the growth hacker is to ruthlessly optimize incoming traffic for success. As Eric Ries explains in *The Lean Startup*, "The focus needs to be on improving customer retention." Forget the conventional wisdom that says if a company lacks growth, it should invest more in sales and marketing. Instead, it should invest in refining and improving the service itself until users are so happy that they can't stop using the service (and their friends come along with them).

This should come as a major relief to marketers—I know it did for me. It means that we don't have to do all the heavy lifting. Instead, we can lean on and work with other facets of the company to make sure that lead generation is actually leading to sales.

Doing this can be incredibly low-tech, as I personally experienced when I signed up for a new service called DogVacay. Like Airbnb for dogs, it helps pet owners find neighbors and nearby animal lovers willing to be pet sitters—instead of having to send their dogs to the kennel while on a trip.

My girlfriend and I excitedly signed up one day after reading about DogVacay on a blog and then promptly forgot all about it. About three days later, we received an unexpected phone call. It was someone from the Dog-Vacay team, wondering what had happened and if there was anything they could do. The caller walked us through the service again, helped us complete our profile, and got us set up with our first host. It wasn't exactly a scalable strategy—if they had a million users they couldn't call each one—but it did, in my case, turn a looky-loo into an active user. And that meant one less new customer who had to be acquired via other means. (Of course I also told everyone I knew about this customer service experience.)

For the same reason, I love the idea of Dropbox rewarding users with 250 megabytes of extra storage if they take a tour of the basics of Dropbox. The idea is to teach members how to use the service and motivate them to get past potential hurdles. It's also why the site offers a 125-megabyte bonus to users who send Dropbox just ninety characters of feedback about the service—now they're involved and participating. (Personally, I've earned something like 625 megabytes of free space, which makes me a happier user, more likely to refer friends, and keeps me "stuck" to the service. It's the kind of marketing that, just a year ago, I'd never have considered marketing.)

In the course of the millions of ad impressions I generated over my traditional marketing career, I never followed up with anyone who converted and I spent only a few seconds thinking about the people who didn't convert at all. I—along with everyone in my industry—was obsessed with more, more, more instead of getting the most out of the leads we were already generating. It makes me shudder to think of the wasted effort inherent in that approach.

SCALING RETENTION AND OPTIMIZATION

Of course, retaining and improving the experience of your incoming customers does not need to involve individually calling each potential customer.

I'll give you another example. In 2011 or 2012, I was invited to be an early user of Uber in Los Angeles. I signed up but for some reason never ended up actually using it to ride anywhere. To use the technical term, I "bounced" out of the service. So I knew of the service, but I was not a user.

Flash forward to a year later, when I was traveling internationally to attend a conference and the event organizers gave all of the speakers a $50 Uber gift card. (In other words, a viral referral feature.) I couldn't find a cab, so I ended up logging into the app for the first time in many, many months and hailed a black car. As it turned out, the service had been significantly improved. Using it was seamless and enjoyable. After my ride, Uber kept me engaged by asking me to rate my driver, and then it sent me a coupon via e-mail.

Back in the United States a few days later and stranded in Brooklyn, my first thought was, "Let's pull up Uber." I had officially been transformed from a lost customer to an active user.

That is retention and optimization. It is marketing to someone who is a lot more likely to convert than some busy stranger you might otherwise try flashing an online banner ad to.

I also think it's important that Uber was thinking less about how to get *new* users and more about how to drive *revenue* from customers who had already signed up. Remember, raw growth is great, but at the end of the day, we're running businesses here. We want to turn stats into dollars.

None of this is outside your grasp—and it's definitely now part of your job. All marketers have e-mail lists and customer databases. We have plenty of people we have marketed to over the years and—due to problems on *our* end, not theirs—we didn't convert or make the best use of them. Yes, it's more seductive to chase new marketing initiatives. Yes, it would be more fun to get some press. But it's better for business to retain and optimize what we already have.

According to Bain & Company, a 5 percent increase in customer retention can mean a 30 percent increase in profitability for the company. And according to Market

Metrics, the probability of selling to an existing customer is 60 to 70 percent, while to a new prospect it's just 5 to 20 percent.[24] Bronson Taylor, host of *Growth Hacker TV*, puts it in a phrase: "Retention trumps acquisition."[25]

Growth hacking is about maximizing ROI—about expending our energies and efforts where they will be most effective. You're better off rolling out new features that get more out of your customer base, that turn potential users into active users, than going out and pounding the pavement for more potentials. You're better off teaching your customers how to use your product—spending time, as services like Facebook and Amazon do, to get users to supply more personal information and make them more engaged—than chasing some new person who doesn't really care.

The logic here should sound familiar. It goes way back to before growth hacking. It's an eternal truth of the human experience. A bird in the hand, remember, is worth two in the bush.

MY CONVERSION: PUTTING THE LESSONS INTO PRACTICE

> We might not have marketing budgets, or a massive fan base. . . . [But] we can build books for sharing. We can sample at scale. We can give readers a stake in distribution. We can open up exchange between artist and fan, beyond the sales transaction. And we can do this in a way that drives creative profitability.
>
> —MATT MASON, CHIEF CONTENT OFFICER,
> BITTORRENT

My fascination with growth hacking began with a wake-up call. I read Andrew Chen's article, and it pierced the bubble I was living in. My job—in fact, the job of all VPs of marketing—was under siege. It made it clear to me that the industry was changing, that a group of thinkers and entrepreneurs was disrupting my field from the outside and I ought to monitor the situation closely.

By late 2012, it was an awakening I was very glad I'd had. Because I found myself in a situation not unlike that of many start-ups. One of the authors I had the privilege of working with, bestseller Tim Ferriss, was suddenly deprived of many of the most effective channels of book marketing. We (along with Amazon, his publisher) were caught by surprise when nearly every retail outlet, from Barnes & Noble to your corner bookstore, refused to carry his third book, *The 4-Hour Chef*—or any other book published by Amazon. We were faced with what should have been an impossible task: promoting a book when all of the traditional avenues were closed. (Oh, and we had less than sixty days to do it all.)

My job was to help make it a bestseller. This was, in many ways, the perfect opportunity for me to try many of the things I had only been able to read about.

We had to be creative. We had to be analytical. We had to think outside the box. We had to use our relatively limited resources extremely carefully. We treated the book as a start-up and growth hacked accordingly.

It was a far cry from the old model: get reviewed in the *New York Times*, pay for shelf space at the front of Barnes & Noble or Books-A-Million, and wait for success (which may never come).

But thanks to the new mindset, I was calm. Out of this seemingly negative situation came one of the most successful launches I have ever been a part of. The book debuted on every bestseller list from the *New York Times* to *USA Today* and hit the number one spot on the *Wall Street Journal*. Even without a presence in brick-and-mortar retail outlets, *The 4-Hour Chef* sold more than sixty thousand *physical* copies in its first week. It was an astounding success.

From my reading and interviews, I had seen that growth hacking could be powerful. Seeing it in action was something else entirely.

Here are some of the things we did.

PRODUCT MARKET FIT

Rather than making a big, general book that appealed to no one, Tim took Product Market Fit to the next level—designing each chapter to stand alone on its own merits and made specifically for a defined community and group of readers. Even within the chapters, he wanted bite-size pieces of content that would immediately provide value to the reader—if you picked up the book and opened it to a random page, he wanted you to be able to get something out of it.

Even Tim's editing was data-driven. Though the final book was roughly six hundred pages long, the early drafts were much closer to eight hundred. Those cuts weren't made by gut instinct, but methodically. Tim used tools like SurveyMonkey and Wufoo to ask friends and colleagues about the sections they responded to most. We tested the back cover and subtitle repeatedly. Before a section was cut or added, multiple readers of the manuscript had to agree.

The result was a book perfectly crafted for its prospective readers, one that we knew would spread and generate reactions because this had been built into the writing itself. The product and the market were in sync.

GROWTH AND ATTENTION

Instead of pushing for TV and radio coverage, we worked with bloggers—because blogs are trackable and work fast. Knowing the type of reach we needed, we set a floor: the blogs had to have more than one hundred thousand unique visitors a month. With tools like Compete, Quantcast, and Alexa, it was easy to research potential sites we wanted to appear on, cross-check their traffic, and then reach out. And as I explained earlier, when your product is actually relevant and designed for a specific audience, bloggers *love* to write about you. Writing articles about you means more pageviews (and advertising revenue) for them!

The result was big online media mentions we scheduled to go live the day of release in a well-timed barrage: *Lifehacker. The Art of Manliness. AskMen. Epic Meal Time.* These hits drove real sales that we tracked with affiliate links.

Blogs were just one part. We partnered with startups, with apps, with anyone who had an audience.

Of course, a major benefit to promoting this book was that Tim had already built a platform. How much easier would it be for anyone to launch a new product if they spent the time developing and building an audience beforehand? For Tim, blogging weekly for five years meant he had a captive audience to launch to, and this was a huge asset for us.

Before you say that's unfair, ask yourself, what's stopping you from developing your own? If you're planning to launch a business in a few months or a few years, start building your platform—and your network—today. It will make your launch, as it did for Tim, much much easier.

VIRALITY

The virality aspect is the part of the launch we're the most proud of. Forced to innovate, we reached out to BitTorrent, where a friend of mine, Matt Mason, had recently taken a job. The team's proposal was audacious: creating a bundle of content from the book to be given away to BitTorrent's 170 million members.

With BitTorrent we produced a slick 700-megabyte bundle—more than 250 pages of material, interviews, extras, videos, and photos—and it was totally free and could be downloaded by anyone. It was the ultimate "try it before you buy it" marketing mechanism. The sales prompt inside of it? A link to buy the book for up to 40 percent off at Amazon.

The results stunned even us:

- **2,000,000 downloads**
- **1,261,152 page visits**
- **880,009 Amazon impressions**
- **327,555 Tim Ferriss website impressions**
- **293,936 book trailer impressions**

I can't disclose actual sales data, but this translated into thousands and thousands of copies sold.

Part of the reason for the success of the promotion, in my view, is that it solved a critical problem in the book discovery process. A lot of books get good publicity and then slam these leads into the brick wall of a $20 price point. It's tough for a book to go viral. This collaboration changed that. People could take a chance on the book, and they could send a link to their friends, who could in turn download the bundle for free.

The BitTorrent promo was undoubtedly the most effective part of the launch.

Later Tim ended up coming back to this well for a further viral lift. He actually gave away a free download of *The 4-Hour Chef* audiobook on BitTorrent along with a bunch of other bonuses.

The audiobook download—because it was free and easily shareable—did more than twenty-five million impressions. Three million of those people downloaded the book, and 117,000 of them gave an e-mail address that Tim would later market to. Overall, sales of Tim's book—in hardcover and digital—rose 5 percent (his Amazon rank alone jumped 394 points).[26]

OPTIMIZATION AND RETENTION

A printed book is not an easy thing to "optimize." Once it's written and printed—at least at the time of this writing—you can't easily change it. It's "done" in the way that an app or a website needn't be. But even so, the optimization and retention approach of growth hacking was influential in this product launch.

In most launches I've been a part of, the mindset

is simple: get as much publicity and attention as you can, and afterward hope or assume it was all a success. Tim's data-driven approach, however, meant we actually looked at what worked and what didn't. We weren't chasing vanity metrics. If the BitTorrent promotion hadn't driven sales, I wouldn't have told you about it.

In fact, based on the success of that collaboration, I worked with BitTorrent again with another client, the musician Alex Day. His results were equally stunning: 2,765,023 downloads, 276,409 page visits, 166,638 iTunes impressions, 52,151 Alex Day website impressions, and 5,000 new e-mail sign-ups for Alex's mailing list.

And we know what worked and what didn't because we pored over the analytics. We looked at which blog posts worked and which didn't, which drove traffic and which didn't, what drove spikes in Amazon rank and what didn't. This information will be crucial in subsequent launches and, of course, with my other clients.

THE FUTURE OF MARKETING

If you know the Way broadly you will see it in everything.

—MIYAMOTO MUSASHI

If something as old-school as publishing can be invigo-rated by the growth hacker approach, what else can? If you can treat a book like a start-up, anything is game.

Whether we're marketing a car or a movie or a small restaurant, have the ability to put these tactics into prac-tice. We're no longer dependent on a guessing game. We don't have to pay outsiders to represent our product—we don't have to buy their relationships with the media.

Instead, we can grow our businesses by iterating, by tracking success, by doing whatever we can to bring people into our sales funnel. And then we understand that it's up to us to optimize our product around these customers and their needs. We can change on the fly. We can spend our budgets on product improvements instead of additional advertising.

You will find, as I did, that the definition of *marketing* is in desperate need of expansion. In fact, anything and everything can be considered marketing—so long as it grows the business.

Before he became the most brilliant and famous man in the ad business, David Ogilvy sold ovens door-to-door. Because of that, he never forgot that advertising is just a slightly more scalable form of creating demand than door-to-door sales.

But far too many of us in the marketing world, decades away from a world of traveling salesmen and mail-order catalogs, have lost sight of this fundamental reality. We forget the function behind the form and miss out on new opportunities because we can't see what's in front of us. At the core, marketing is lead generation. Ads drive awareness . . . to drive sales. PR and publicity drive attention . . . to drive sales. Social media drives communication . . . to drive sales. Marketing, too many people forget, is not an end unto itself. It is simply getting customers. And by the transitive property, *anything that gets customers is marketing.*

That is what growth hackers have taught us.

Run down the list of the start-ups we've talked about in this book, from Hotmail to Airbnb to Groupon to Spotify, and see the startling fact: tactics that no one would have previously described as "marketing" turned out to be the marketing steroids behind their business growth. For Hotmail, it was inserting an e-mail signature at the bottom of each message that turned every e-mail sent by one of its users into a pitch for new users. For Airbnb, it was craigslist infiltration, which allowed Airbnb hosts to use the site as a sales platform. For Groupon and Living-Social, it was their referral offers that paid users to share deals with their friends. And for Spotify, it was the free "advertising" it got from Facebook integration.

More important than any of their specific tactics was the mindset they all shared. Each followed the process I've outlined in this book: they merged marketing into their product development; they kicked off growth with early adopters; they added viral elements; and then they relentlessly repeated these cycles, always guided by the data, with an eye toward optimization.

Their innovative approaches to growth were possible because they came from start-ups, businesses typically averse to traditional marketing for two reasons: they don't have the money and they don't have the experience. Because these companies didn't have access to the "luxuries" of an ad budget or the burden of proper training, they were able to be creative enough to broaden the definition of *marketing* to immense advantage. Meanwhile, companies with the ability to spend millions a year (or month) chug along with poorer results and poorer ROI.

The thing about marketers—and, well, everyone—is that we're wrong *all the time*. We think we make good gut decisions, but we don't. The old model makes being wrong incredibly expensive. Who can afford to learn that the product isn't resonating *after* they've spent months planning a campaign? Growth hacking doesn't make our instincts any better, but it fundamentally reduces the costs of being wrong, giving us freedom to experiment and try new things.

We no longer have an excuse for expensive, indulgent mistakes. The alternative is too easy and too reliable.

As I interviewed and read about the dozens of growth hackers whose many insights contributed to this book, I noticed that each one had used an almost entirely different set of tactics than the others. Some had relied on viral features; others leaned more heavily on product and optimization. Some were expert e-mail marketers, while others knew how to use platforms and APIs to reach equally large amounts of people.

For all the tactical differences, the strategic goal was the same: to reach people in an effective, scalable, and data-driven way. Granted, it didn't always look or feel cool and *Mad Men*–esque, like retaining a creative agency, seeing your billboards around town, or pulling in celebrity endorsements does. But the difference is that those things don't guarantee success anymore. And they cost fifty to a hundred times more.

Growth hacking really is a mindset rather than a tool kit. And if you leave this book with one thing, it should be that mindset.

Once you break out of the shackles of antiquated notions of what is or isn't marketing, the whole field becomes cheaper, easier, and much more scalable. The game changes forever.

It gets exponentially better.

SPECIAL BONUS

If you would like the raw transcripts of the interviews I did with the world's best growth hackers for this book, along with the research and materials I gathered, I'd like to send them to you.

All you need to do is send an e-mail here: growthhackermarketing@gmail.com.

I will also send you a chapter from my first book, *Trust Me, I'm Lying: Confessions of a Media Manipulator*, which shows you how to get free publicity and press. As a bonus I'll give you a redemption code for one month of free membership to Growth Hacker TV (a $29 value), which has hundreds of video interviews from the people who built everything from Facebook to the *Huffington Post* to Etsy.

AFTERWORD

I am in the lucky position of being able to update this book for its expanded paperback edition. Instead of using that opportunity to simply retread old ground, I thought I would add a few additional lessons I learned growth hacking the book you just read.

After all, my advice and recommendations wouldn't be worth much if I hadn't followed them myself. Can you imagine if I had promoted this book about growth hacking using anything but the tactics in this book? Though I learned some lessons from the Tim Ferriss launch, this book was an opportunity for me to apply the science from day one with complete control.

STEP 1

This book didn't start as a book. It started as a minimum viable product—a short, one-thousand-word article for

Fast Company, in fact. The response to that article led to interest from Penguin (my publisher), but instead of following the traditional publishing playbook (it takes about fourteen months to produce a physical book) we started by publishing a digital single right away. Publishing *Growth Hacker Marketing* as a short eBook drastically reduced our cost and let us test the market, and more important, beat our competitors to market. The fact that many people are reading this book in print right now is because that experiment—that minimum viable product test—was validated.

I was then able to edit, improve, and add to the original text of the eBook for the version you're now reading. Based on the feedback of the thousands of original readers, I'm able to produce a better, more marketable product to ideally take this project to the next level. Now we can have our big launch because we know the audience is there.

I know this probably seems basic, but traditional publishing is a business that regularly gives six-figure, even seven-figure advances based simply on book *proposals*, even though most books never earn back that money. Doing it this way was a huge step forward, and I think it's something that all authors or businesspeople can learn from.

Lesson: Cheaply test your concept, improve it based on feedback, then launch.

STEP 2

I think the best growth hack we had for this book was something that was actually brought up during the contract negotiations. What would we price it at?

My last book sold for $26.95 hardcover and $12.99 as an eBook. I don't think that did a first-time author like myself any favors in the acquiring customers department. So the digital single for this book was $2.99. That meant basically *anyone* could afford to give it a read. By making the cost really low and then overdelivering on content we set this book up to succeed.

I had some other great hacks, too. Before launch I wrote approximately a dozen articles by adapting lessons and content from the book for publication on influential sites. Instead of charging for my writing as I usually do, I gave these away for free.

The result was popular articles on MarketWatch, Betabeat, *Fast Company*, *Thought Catalog*, *The Huffington Post*, Shopify, *Hacker News*, SlideShare.com, reddit, Medium, and a few others. This content marketing strategy is now quite common in the start-up space because it's cheap and available to anyone who can write decently.

I also relied on my own ten-thousand-person mailing list, which I had built slowly over the past six years painstakingly recommending books by *other authors*. This list has some of the most die-hard book fans and rabid readers you can imagine. (For anyone who wants to sign up, you can do so here: http://www.ryanholiday.net/reading-newsletter.)

Finally, I reached out to the growth hacker community, who was looking for a book that validated and championed its work. The most influential guys in the space, from Sean Ellis to Andrew Chen, all helped promote the book to their audiences on Twitter and Facebook, which helped get this project going.

Lesson: Reduce barriers to entry; use targeted media and platforms to bring your first users on board.

STEP 3

Aside from the price, which I think made this book much easier to spread by word of mouth, I designed this book to be viral. (Again, creating a positive disparity between price expectation and the product you deliver is important. It means people say things like, "I can't believe this is *only* three dollars.")

One look at the Amazon page tells me we were successful. Hundreds and hundreds of Kindle and Goodreads readers have bookmarked, tweeted, and shared passages they liked. That's not an accident.

When I was writing I tried to keep my sentences short and make my revelations big and exciting. I wanted people to leave with important and actionable sound bites. And I did even more of this for the new version.

The articles and content I produced for the book had the same effect. It's a lot easier to share a blog post—which in my case were basically advertisements for the longer book.

Lesson: Aim for a *wow* factor and response from your customers.

STEP 4

The shame of most authors is that they have no way of reaching their fans. They start every project from scratch. I didn't want to do that with this new edition. So I added a small page to the digital single that gave away a plethora of bonuses for readers. All they had to do was e-mail growthhackermarketing@gmail.com. (This bonus still works if you want it!)

About 10 percent of all readers did this—which is a great conversion rate. I made those readers extra happy and satisfied by giving them free stuff. But most important, I built an e-mail list of my most interested readers.

Now, I can alert them about the new, expanded version of this book. I can tell them that it's now available in paperback (which many people had asked about). I can even tell them about other books I wrote.

I worked hard to convert those people into paying customers; I would have been an idiot if I let them walk out the door without at least trying to get their contact info. That's true for any project, no matter what we're doing. You've got to build a list, because a list is the easiest and most effective marketing tool, period.

Of course, for step 4 I also had another luxury most authors never get. I got to incorporate real reader feedback into the project. Launching with a short digital version first meant I could optimize and improve based on the responses from those original readers. The book you've just read is not only 30 percent longer, but it's packed with new examples, better writing, and fewer (ideally, no) errors.

Lesson: Build your e-mail list!

CONCLUSION

I don't want to belabor the point. I understand that not everyone markets books and not everyone is publishing one these days (even though it feels like it sometimes).

But I wanted to show how simple it is to apply the growth hacker mindset to *any* project. And how if you do it long enough it basically becomes a habit. I can tell you that the launch of this book—and the launch of the edition you just read—was one of the least stressful and yet most effective launches I've ever done.

It didn't feel like I was *selling*, because I wasn't. I wasn't *pushing*, because I didn't need to. I'd built those aspects into the product. I'd hacked marketing and product development and sales together into a perpetual motion machine. And there is nothing I did here that couldn't be applied to your own book, to your start-up, to that new project you're launching at the company you work for. It's infinitely malleable and applicable.

Of course whether you do so is up to you. All I can say is that I never want to do it the old way again. Because this, well, it just works.

A GROWTH HACKING GLOSSARY

As a tech- and data-driven mindset, growth hacking can be intimidating to beginners. That growth hacking helped build Dropbox and Airbnb and Facebook is clear and obvious to even the most novice observer. But when you start to dig into the specifics—the how and the why—your eyes are likely to glaze over. What is "cohort analysis"? What's a "viral coefficient"? While researching for this book over the past year, I've tried to come up with some definitions for the core concepts of growth hacking—if only for my own use and reference.

Adding these words to your vocabulary will not only make the concepts and principles of growth hacking clearer but they should also hopefully help you parse through the excellent and high-level advice of the growth hackers who blog and share their secrets.

Here you go.

A/B testing *(v.)*—A/B testing is just what it sounds like. You create two versions of a website or product, show them to people, and see which does better—A or B? From Google to Qualaroo to Optimizely to KISSmetrics, there are great services that allow you to see what your users are actually doing and responding to on your site. This *objective* insight will get you closer to a fit than gut instincts ever will.

bootstrapping *(v.)*—Bootstrapping is a method of funding a business, usually a tech start-up, that doesn't take in any outside funding and therefore runs on an extremely tight budget. In today's tech culture of celebrating huge fund-raising from venture capitalists, bootstrapping should be a badge of honor. When you are bootstrapping, you pay for your own marketing, or, your marketing pays for itself. This means using growth hacker tactics to acquire your users to find ways to increase each dollar your customer spends with you. GitHub, 37signals, and AppSumo are all examples of extremely successful companies that bootstrapped and never took venture capital along the way.

bounce rate *(n.)*—Bounce rate is the objective measure of your stickiness. (You can get it from Google Analytics or KISSmetrics or any such service.) When a user goes to your site, what percentage of them immediately leave? If that percentage is high—and it is often much, much too high—you've got one of two problems. A) Your website or service sucks. (See: Product Market Fit.) B) You're chasing the wrong kind of users, probably using expensive traditional marketing techniques. To improve your bounce rate, you need to either adjust the service—iteratively, using A/B testing—or adjust who you are trying to attract to your service. If people are coming to your site and only a small percentage "stay," the answer is never, I repeat, never, to try to get high volumes of traffic. (Don't try to get featured on *TechCrunch again* just because it was only mildly lucrative the first time.) It is far easier and more effective to improve your bounce rate.

cohort analysis *(n.)*—A cohort analysis uses data from a web application and separates it into related groups of people, rather than just looking at all customers as a whole. Cohort analysis allows you to look at the entire life cycle of specific groups of customers, which allows businesses to make different offerings to specific people.

Growth hackers use cohort analyses to track specific users from first contact through the sales funnel to give segments of users what they are looking for.

conversion rate *(n.)*—In simple terms, this is the number of people who see your product or site divided by the number of people who perform your desired action (signing up, buying, entering their e-mail address, etc.). Growth hackers obsess about conversion rate.

At the end of the day, growth hackers don't care about "awareness" or "attention" or "mind share." They care about *acquiring users*. That means they care about conversion rate above basically everything else. This shift is crucial. After all, what's the point of driving a bunch of new visitors to your website if they don't perform the action you drove them there to perform?

growth hacker (*n.*)—A growth hacker is an employee with a simple job: growing the business by any means possible. This role, according to Andrew Chen and many Silicon Valley pioneers, has come to supplant the typical VP of Marketing. Growth hackers' main task is to build great marketing ideas into the product during the development process. Growth hackers often have a programming background, but it's not required. Growth hackers are pros at hypothesizing, testing, and iterating different versions of their products to create hockey stick growth for their companies. Examples include Noah Kagan, who was a growth hacker at Facebook and Mint.com before he started AppSumo, which he grew from a sixty-dollar investment to a seven-figure business; or Sean Ellis, who developed the referral program for Dropbox (which drove millions of new users) and is now the CEO at Qualaroo and an advisor to other start-ups.

growth hacking *(v.)*—Growth hacking is business strategy that throws out the playbook of traditional marketing and replaces it with customer acquisition techniques that are testable, trackable, and scalable. Its tools are e-mails, pay-per-click ads, blogs, and platform APIs instead of commercials, publicity, and money. While traditional marketing chases vague notions like "branding" and "mind share," growth hackers relentlessly pursue users and growth—and when they do it right, those users beget more users, who beget more users. They are the inventors, operators, and mechanics of their own self-sustaining and self-propagating growth machine that can take a start-up from nothing to *something*.

minimum viable product *(n.)*—A minimum viable product is an early, bare-bones version of a product that allows founders to collect meaningful data about their (potential) customers quickly and with little effort. Eric Ries, author of *The Lean Startup*, explains that the best way to get to Product Market Fit is by starting with an "MVP" and improving it based on feedback—as opposed to what many traditional marketers do, which is to try to launch with what we think is our final product. Isolating who your customers are, figuring out their needs, designing a product that will blow their minds—these are marketing decisions, not just development and design choices. At

Amazon, for instance, product managers must submit press releases to their supervisors before the development team even starts working on it. That exercise forces the team to focus on the market for the new product and what's special about it.

pivot *(v.)*—Eric Ries defines a pivot as a "structured course correction designed to test a new fundamental hypothesis about the product, strategy, and engine of growth." In other words, tweaking or changing your product because customers aren't responding like you thought. Instagram started as a geo-location start-up called Burbn but changed to become Instagram as we know it—a mobile app for posting photos with filters—after tailoring its app to focus on the features that users responded to. The result? One hundred thousand users within a week of relaunching. Within eighteen months, the founders sold Instagram for $1 billion. That's a pivot.

Product Market Fit *(n.)*—Product Market Fit is the achievement of a state in which a product and its customers are in perfect sync with one another. This is the holy grail for every growth hacker. Growth hackers believe that products—even whole businesses and business models—can and should be changed until they are primed to generate explosive reactions from the first people who see them. In other words, the best marketing decision you can make is to have a product or business that fulfills a real and compelling need for a real and defined group of people—no matter how much tweaking and refining this takes. They treat their products and services as something malleable and are able to change and improve them until they find the best iterations.

(publicity) stunt *(n.)*—A stunt is a way to get people talking about—or trying—a new product. Sometimes "stunts" are a great way to get users—they are growth hacks that kick-start the whole process. Publicity stunts are often about exploiting systems or platforms that others have not yet fully appreciated. Uber has used publicity stunts to create viral attention and disrupt the entire taxi industry. For example, the Uber team provided roses free of charge on Valentine's Day to users looking to impress their dates. They even partnered with ice cream trucks to bring users treats via their app and signed a deal to give cheap rides to NFL players who kept getting DUIs.

sales funnel *(n.)*—A sales funnel is a series of steps to find leads and direct them through the sales process, with the end goal of converting as many of those leads into paying customers. For example, Mint.com baked lead generation directly into their application. At the top of their sales funnel are all the free users, who gladly signed up for Mint.com's amazing and fast personal finance application. Mint.com then partnered with financial services companies to act as an affiliate by allowing them to offer good deals to the users of Mint.com's free services.

Other growth hackers like Noah Kagan at AppSumo give their customers huge discounts on related products after they make a purchase, thus engineering more up-sells and drawing users deeper into the funnel.

stickiness *(adj.)*—The stickiness of a service or product can be thought of as how likely someone is to buy your product repeatedly or recommend it to others. According to Chip and Dan Heath's *Made to Stick*, sticky ideas and products tend to be simple, unexpected, and credible, with concrete details, an emotional undertow, and a memorable story line. Growth hacking extends this definition to services and platforms. When someone signs up, do they become active users? Or do they immediately quit and leave? When someone checks out your app, are they drawn into it, or is the reaction more of a "meh"? When Twitter rolled out its Suggested Users list feature, it helped new members stick to the service because now they had interesting friends to follow. The services that suck you in and keep you there—they are sticky.

vanity metrics *(n.)*—Vanity metrics are the metrics that *feel* important but are ultimately superficial or, worse, deceptive. For instance, monitoring traffic to your website (congratulating yourself that it is increasing) while ignoring conversion rate, bounce rate, time on site, and so forth, would be falling prey to a vanity metric.

"Vanity metrics are the numbers you want to publish on *TechCrunch* to make your competitors feel bad," says Eric Ries. But their usefulness ends there.

Vanity metrics are measurements that paint a rosy picture for a start-up but aren't actionable. Measuring your company using vanity metrics may allow you to boast about how many users you have on your blog, but the cost of acquiring those users may lead you to ruin if you're not careful. Techniques like A/B testing can provide you with actionable metrics because you will be able to *replicate* the results.

viral loop *(n.)*—A viral loop is the process by which a person goes from seeing your product or service to using it and sharing it with others. For example, let's say your friend gets an e-mail from his favorite product asking him to join a contest. He joins and shares it on Twitter because the product offers him another entry if he does. You see your friend's tweet and click on it, entering the contest as well and sharing it with even more people. This is how viral loops become self-contained, self-fueling mechanisms of growth. Facebook newsfeeds and embeddable YouTube videos are all great examples of viral loops.

virality (and viral coefficient) *(n.)*—Virality is the person-to-person spread of a product or an idea. Because growth hacking is about scalability—ideally you want your marketing efforts to bring in users, which then bring in more users—it often depends on viral techniques for growth. Virality at its core is asking someone to spend their social capital recommending or linking or posting about you for *free*. But virality is not an accident. It is *engineered*. And it goes without saying why viral spread is critical to the growth hacker approach.

Ideally, growth hackers look for a viral coefficient (or "K factor") greater than one. The term "K factor" is typically used in medicine to describe the contagion of disease. In the start-up world, the viral coefficient measures the number of new users that each existing user is able to convert. If each new user is bringing in, on average, more than one user, then the K factor is greater than one and your start-up is going viral.

A product or business or piece of content will go viral only if it provokes a desire in people to spread it. On top of that, a growth hacker must facilitate and encourage its spread by adding tools and campaigns that enable virality. All of which is to say a simple truth that we try to deny too often: if you want to go viral, virality must be baked into your product.

FAQS

The following are answers to the more frequently asked questions that I received since publication of the book, via e-mail and Twitter, as well as during an "Ask Me Anything" (AMA) I did on reddit. I'm happy to answer them because many of the questions mirror exactly my initial queries to the growth hackers during my interviews and research for the book itself.

1. **If you were launching a start-up or new product, what questions would you ask yourself before launching?**

   I'd ask myself:

   - Who are my ideal early adopters?
   - How can I make my platform particularly enticing to them right now?

- Why is this service indispensable? Or how do I make it indispensable to them?
- Once they come on board, does the service provide/encourage/facilitate them inviting or bringing more users with them?
- How willing and prepared am I to improve based on the feedback and behavior of these users?
- What kind of crazy/cool thing can I do to get attention—something that, ideally, no one has ever done before?

2. Isn't growth hacker marketing just an evolution of traditional marketing?

It is not in the marketing industry's DNA to be any of the following things, which are critical to growth hacking:

- In-house
- Lean/efficient
- Trackable
- Internal (that is product development) over external (public facing/attention seeking)

Traditional marketing strategies simply weren't used to build companies like Facebook, Airbnb, and Twitter, and they're some of the fastest-growing companies in the world. They also weren't built simply with direct marketing strategies like e-mail or standard mail. It was all of these things combined but used and deployed in a new way.

This presents a great opportunity for prospective growth hackers. They can dominate the marketing industry going forward as the giants grow less and less effective.

3. What are some key strategies to acquire your first 100K users with zero marketing budget?

The best strategic marketing decision you can make is to have a product or business fulfill a real, compelling need for a real and defined group of people—no matter how much tweaking and refining this takes. You don't get 100K users with zero marketing budget unless you've got an amazing product that fills a real and compelling need *right now*. Think: Snapchat, Instagram, or even Zappos. While these companies did something very different from one another, they really made people say *wow*. It's that reaction that does your marketing for you and drives word of mouth.

Rather than wait for this to magically happen, you need to contribute to this process.

Ask yourself: why would anyone sign up for a beta list for a new product or sign up the week it launches? The value proposition has to be overwhelming—as it was for Dropbox, for Mailbox, and for Gmail. These services blew up because the reaction they elicited was "Holy shit." Same goes for most of the cool Kickstarter projects you see (in which case people are basically pre-ordering a product they've never seen and that might never actually exist).

If your product does not do that—even on a small scale for a much smaller audience—you need to go back to the drawing board until it does. All the important things that follow, like getting press and influencer attention, are impossible until this is obtained.

Your outward-facing marketing and PR efforts are simply to reach out to and capture, at the beginning, a group of highly interested, loyal, and fanatical users. Then you grow with and because of them. Product Market Fit is not some mythical status that happens accidentally. Companies work for it, they crawl toward it. They're ready to throw out weeks or months of work because the evidence supports that decision.

4.   **What are some good resources to use when doing market research for a start-up or industry?**

Aside from studying your competition and reading the blogs and thought leaders in your space? One of my favorite tricks: Find a subreddit (a topic-driven niche on the reddit site that addresses the market or space you plan to launch in), subscribe, and watch the articles (and the comments to those articles) for a few weeks.* See what people say, what they react to, what they like and dislike, etc.

Unfortunately, when it comes to market research I feel it's less about the tools and more about the effort. How much time do you put in? How willing are you to actually *listen* to the feedback around you? Are you falling prey to the confirmation bias? All those factors will ultimately matter more than whether you use a Wufoo forum to ask users some questions.

5. **Do you feel building virality into the product should be done only after finding Product Market Fit?**

I don't think these are totally distinct things. Product Market Fit is itself a viral component. You're making something that people *want and need*. That being said, using an example like Dropbox, clearly their "Get free space" referral program would not have worked if Product Market Fit wasn't there also. It's a chicken-and-egg problem—so

---

* For a searchable list, just go here: http://www.reddit.com/reddits.

don't think about the order necessarily, but make sure you have the framework for both.

6.   **I've seen the writing on the wall as you have about traditional marketing strategies paling in comparison to growth hacking. I have traditional marketing experience but I want to transition into working as a growth hacker. How do I do it?**

Find a start-up that could use your skills and offers the opportunity to experiment with some of these newer strategies. Or better yet, find stuff you're passionate about, look for people who are doing the coolest stuff in that space, and find a way that you can bring something to the table that they want. You can get the mindset for growth hacking by reading. You learn the techniques by doing.

7.   **I'm looking to build buzz around a physical product I'm working on and am considering making content to advertise to my target de-mographic. What do I need to think about?**

Put yourself in the viewers' shoes. Why would they watch your content? The proposition is: here, click this ad to watch a video about some product you've never heard of. Not that exciting, right? Try to change that up and you'll have more luck. How can you make the content good enough and valuable enough that you don't need ads to be the main driver of views? Honestly, the best way to build buzz around a physical product is probably in person, where the physical attributes can actually be experienced. But if you're going to make content and you want it to work, make sure it is compelling and emphasizes the attributes that separate your product from the herd.

8. What are your thoughts on traditional advertising and PR agencies?

If I were in PR, I'd quit because it sucks. It's a bunch of relationships with people who don't matter that much anymore (i.e., legacy media reporters).

As far as ad agencies go, I don't like their model. Why do you have to pay someone else to make/produce the content that you use to *speak directly to your potential customers*? It makes no sense to me. That being said, I think there is a lot of value in learning what those guys do and then applying it on your own to a company where you actually work or control things.

As an alternative, I'd focus on helping people do

really cool, interesting things and media attention will not only follow, it will pound down your door.

9. **Do I have to run a tech start-up to use growth hacking strategies, or will they work for other types of professions and businesses? For example, accountants, lawyers, or a physical product like a toaster? What about B2B?**

The growth hacker mindset still applies no matter what kind of business you're in: make your service indispensable, find some loophole or underexploited niche, encourage word of mouth, and finally, ruthlessly optimize based on data and feedback.

Growth hacking a social network to millions of users is impressive—but it's always going to be a little easier to acquire users for a free product than it is going to be to acquire *customers* and clients. But you can ultimately apply these tactics—likely on a smaller scale—to all sorts of businesses, be they physical products or restaurants or whatever.

This is precisely why I concluded the book with an example of growth hacking a book. I wanted to show that applying the process is what matters—not the product. After all, Aaron Ginn worked as a growth hacker for a presidential campaign in 2012. I think we can safely say that you ought to be able to apply it to your Indiegogo campaign or even a charity. As they say in AA, the steps work if you work them.

10. **What books would you recommend to an aspiring entrepreneur?**

Some quick favorites:

The 22 Immutable Laws of Marketing: Violate Them at Your Own Risk! by Al Ries and Jack Trout

The 48 Laws of Power by Robert Greene

The 33 Strategies of War by Robert Greene

Antifragile: Things That Gain from Disorder by Nassim Nicholas Taleb

The Fish That Ate the Whale: The Life and Times of America's Banana King by Rich Cohen

Wikinomics: How Mass Collaboration Changes Everything by Don Tapscott and Anthony D. Williams

Contagious: Why Things Catch On by Jonah Berger

The Pirate's Dilemma: How Youth Culture Is Reinventing Capitalism by Matt Mason

Rules for Radicals: A Pragmatic Primer for Realistic Radicals by Saul D. Alinsky

The New New Thing: A Silicon Valley Story by Michael Lewis

Here Comes Everybody: The Power of Organizing Without Organizations by Clay Shirky

Purple Cow: Transform Your Business by Being Remarkable by Seth Godin

Eleven Rings: The Soul of Success by Phil Jackson and Hugh Delehanty

Billion Dollar Lessons: What You Can Learn from the Most Inexcusable Business Failures of the Last 25 Years by Paul B. Carroll and Chunka Mui

Gonzo Marketing: Winning Through Worst Practices by Christopher Locke

For a more extensive list, check out my monthly recommendations, which I do via e-mail at http://www.ryanholiday .net/reading-newsletter.

BECOMING A
GROWTH HACKER:
THE NEXT STEPS

This book was designed to be an introduction—to convey to you a mindset and a new approach rather than teaching the specific tactics at a granular level. The best way to accomplish that next step is to go directly to the source. By that I mean train under a real growth hacker. No marketer, traditional or otherwise, learned how to do what they *really* do in school. They learned on the job. Thankfully, there are thousands of start-ups and growth companies out there building growth teams right now. And you could get paid to learn and study there.

But if you don't have the time or the access, the following are some amazing resources that pick up where this book leaves off.

BLOGS AND PERSONALITIES

Andrew Chen's essays

> http://andrewchen.co

Noah Kagan's blog

> http://okdork.com

Patrick Vlaskovits

> http://vlaskovits.com/blog
>
> http://www.twitter.com/pv

Jesse Farmer

> http://20bits.com

Sean Ellis

> http://www.startup-marketing
> .com
>
> http://growthhackers.com

Paul Graham's essays

> http://www.paulgraham.com
> /articles.html

Aaron Ginn

> http://www.aginnt.com

Josh Elman

> https://medium.com/@joshelman

Or just follow most of these guys as they answer questions at:

> http://www.quora.com/Growth
> -Hacking

BOOKS

The Lean Startup: How Today's Entrepreneurs Use Continuous Innovation to Create Radically Successful Businesses by Eric Ries

The Lean Entrepreneur: How Visionaries Create Products, Innovate with New Ventures, and Disrupt Markets by Brant Cooper and Patrick Vlaskovits

Founders at Work: Stories of Startups' Early Days by Jessica Livingston

Viral Loop: From Facebook to Twitter, How Today's Smartest Businesses Grow Themselves by Adam L. Penenberg

Lean Startup Marketing: Agile Product Development, Business Model Design, Web Analytics, and other Keys to Rapid Growth by Sean Ellis

PRESENTATIONS, SHOWS, AND CLASSES

http://www.creativelive.com/courses/smart-pr-artists-entrepreneurs-and-small-business-ryan-holiday (a ten-hour course I made with creativeLIVE on marketing, attention, and free publicity)

http://www.slideshare.net/mattangriffel/growth-hacking

http:// quibb. com/ links/growth-hackers
-conference-all-the-lessons-from-every
-presentation

http:// www.slideshare.net/yongfook/growth
-hacking-101-your-first-500000-users

http://www.slideshare.net/gueste94e4c/dropbox
-startup-lessons-learned-3836587

https://www.growthhacker.tv

http://growthhackers.com

http://www.slideshare.net/yongfook/actionable
-growth-hacking-tactics

https://generalassemb.ly/education/growth
-hacking-and-user-acquisition-for
-startups-online-class

https://www.udemy.com/growth-hacking-lean
-marketing-for-startups

http:// www.forbes.com/sites/markfidelman
/2013/10/15/meet-the-growth-hacking
-wizard-behind-facebook-twitter-and
-quoras-astonishing-success/

http:// www. slideshare. net/ vlaskovits
/growthhacker-live-preso-by-patrick
-vlaskovits-pv

http://www.slideshare.net/timhomuth/think
-like-a-growth-hacker

http:// www. slideshare. net/ryanholiday
/19-growth-hacker-quotes

http:// www.slideshare.net/ryanholiday/the
-growth-hacker-wake-up-call

http:// www. slideshare. net/ryanholiday
/10-classic-growth-hacks

http://www.fourhourworkweek.com/blog/2011
/09/24/how-to-create-a-million-dollar
- business- this- weekend- examples
-appsumo-mint-chihuahuas

http://www.growhack.com/case-studies

THERE IS EVEN A GROWTH HACKERS' CONFERENCE

http://growthhackersconference.com

ACKNOWLEDGMENTS

I'd like to thank Samantha Hoover, who patiently helped me research and work on this book. I owe a debt to Brent Underwood and Michael Tunney for their marketing support. Thanks to Milt Deherrera, my man at American Apparel, who ran many of these experiments with me. Thanks to Niki Papadopoulos for spotting the germ of the idea for this book in my *Fast Company* article and to the Portfolio staff and my agent, Steve Hanselman, for bringing it to fruition. Finally, thanks to the growth hackers who taught me and to the readers who provided feedback that took this from a minimum viable product to a bestselling book.

NOTES

1. Andrew Chen, "Growth Hacker Is the New VP Marketing," April 27, 2012, http://andrewchen.co/2012/04/27/how-to-be-a-growth-hacker -an-airbnbcraigslist-case-study.

2. E-mail to author, April 18, 2013.

3. Dialogue from *Viral Loop: From Facebook to Twitter, How Today's Smartest Businesses Grow Themselves* by Adam L. Penenberg (New York: Hyperion, 2009), 96.

4. Kevin J. Clancy and Randy L. Stone, "Don't Blame the Metrics," *Harvard Business Review* (June 2005), http://hbr.org/2005/06/dont -blame-the-metrics/ar/1.

5. E-mail to author, March 18, 2013.

6. Christine Lagorio-Chafkin, "Brian Chesky, Joe Gebbia, and Nathan Blecharczyk, Founders of AirBnB," last updated July 19, 2010, http://www.inc.com/30under30/2010/profile-brian-chesky-joe -gebbia-nathan-blecharczyk-airbnb.html.

7. Laurie Segall, "The Startup That Died So Instagram Could Live," September 13, 2011, http://money.cnn.com/2011/09/13/technology /startups/instagram_burbn/index.htm.

8. You can actually see a basic outline of this press release format on Quora. I highly suggest checking it out at www.quora.com/What-is

-Amazons-approach-to-product-development-and-product-management.

9. Werner Vogels, "Working Backwards," November 1, 2006, www.allthingsdistributed.com/2006/11/working_backwards.html.

10. Marc Andreesen, "Product/Market Fit," June 25, 2007, http://www.stanford.edu/class/ee204/ProductMarketFit.html.

11. Larissa MacFarquhar, "Requiem for a Dream," March 11, 2013, http://www.newyorker.com/reporting/2013/03/11/130311fa_fact_macfarquhar?currentPage=all.

12. Interview with author, May 24, 2013.

13. Chen, "Growth Hacker Is the New VP Marketing."

14. Sean Ellis, "Awareness Building Is a Waste of Startup Resources," March 7, 2008, http://www.startup-marketing.com/awareness-building-is-a-waste-of-startup-resources.

15. Philip Kaplan, "How I Deal with Users Who Steal," updated November 1, 2013, https://medium.com/product-design/416b0841dbf1.

16. Jonah Berger, *Contagious: Why Things Catch On* (New York: Simon & Schuster, 2013), 24.

17. Anthony Ha, "Dropbox CEO: Why Search Advertising Failed Us," October 27, 2010, http://venturebeat.com/2010/10/27/dropbox-drew-houston-adwords/; Drew Houston, "Dropbox Startup Lessons Learned," posted April 24, 2010, http://www.slideshare.net/gueste94e4c/dropbox-startup-lessons-learned-3836587.

18. E-mail to author, March 28, 2013.

19. Richard Price, "Growth Hacking: Leading Indicators of Engaged Users," October 30, 2012, http://www.richardprice.io/post/34652740246/growth-hacking-leading-indicators-of-engaged-users.

20. Cortney Boyd Myers, "Airbnb Launches Its Photography Program

with 13,000 Verified Properties," October 6, 2011, http://thenextweb
.com/apps/2011/10/06/airbnb-launches-its-photography-program-
with-13000-verified-properties/#!pfMjt.

21. E-mail to author, March 28, 2013.

22. Matt Asay, "How Mailbox Scaled to One Million Users in Six Weeks,"
    June 5, 2013, http://readwrite.com/2013/06/05/from-0-to-1-million
    -users-in-six-weeks-how-mailbox-planned-for-scale#awesm
    =~oa92pdwfjg5ExS.

23. Mark Fidelman, "Meet the Growth Hacking Wizard Behind
    Facebook, Twitter and Quora's Astonishing Success," October 15,
    2013, http://www.forbes.com/sites/markfidelman/2013/10/15/meet
    -the-growth-hacking-wizard-behind-facebook-twitter-and-quoras
    -astonishing-success/.

24. April Dunford, "Top 5 Customer Retention Marketing Tactics,"
    May 27, 2010, http://www.rocketwatcher.com/blog/2010/05/top-5
    -customer-retention-marketingtactics.html.

25. Interview with author, April 24, 2013.

26. Porfirio Landeros, "The 4-Hour Chef: What's the Value of a Listen?"
    October 31, 2013, http://blog.bittorrent.com/2013/10/31/the-4-hour
    -chef-whats-the-value-of-a-listen.